SACRED WATER

SACRED WATER

The Spiritual Source of Life

NATHANIEL ALTMAN

HiddenSpring

Jacket design by Per-Henrik Guerth

Book design by Jennifer Ann Daddio

Library of Congress Cataloging-in-Publication Data

Altman, Nathaniel, 1948–
Sacred water : the spiritual source of life / by Nathaniel Altman.
p. cm.
Includes bibliographical references and index.
ISBN 1-58768-013-0 (alk. paper)
1. Water—Mythology. 2. Water—Religious aspects. I. Title.

BL450 .A58 2001
291.1'3—dc21
2001051474

Published by
HiddenSpring
an imprint of Paulist Press
997 Macarthur Boulevard
Mahwah, New Jersey 07430

www.hiddenspringbooks.com

Printed and bound in the United States of America

CONTENTS

SACRED WATER

INTRODUCTION

Be praised, my Lord, through Sister Water,
So very useful, humble, precious and chaste.
—FRANCIS OF ASSISI, FROM
THE CANTICLE OF BROTHER SUN

I have sought the waters today;
we have joined with their sap.
O Agni, full of moisture,
come and flood me with splendor.
—FROM *THE WATERS OF LIFE,*
A HINDU PRAYER

Like many others, my life has always been centered around rivers, lakes, springs, and oceans. I was born in a hospital located along the East River in New York City and grew up in a farmhouse overlooking a tranquil mountain pond that was a favorite spot for fishing and swimming. I chose to attend a university located along the shores of Lake Mendota in Madison, Wisconsin, and spent my senior year living and working in a waterfront apartment with a spectacular view of the lake and surrounding countryside. While working in India after graduating from college, I lived in a house on the Bay of Bengal. With the morning sun reflecting on the sea and the constant rumble of the surf, it was an ongoing source of peace and inspiration. After returning to New York, I spent six months living in an apartment overlooking the Hudson River, and my present home is within a five minute walk of two glacial lakes in Prospect Park, Brooklyn.

My most recent experiences with water took place while writing *Healing Springs,* a book about the medicinal value of hot and mineral springs. Long an enthusiastic devotee of thermal waters, I was able to visit spas in the United States, Europe, and Asia in the course of my research. I always feel at home in a water environment and have grown to appreciate the vital role that water plays in my existence. As a *living substance* that is the foundation of all life processes on Earth, water is not an ordinary commodity but something marvelous, magical, and sacred.

WHAT MAKES WATER SACRED?

Because it is so essential to life, water is the primordial element underlying myths and legends around the world. Early Egyptian creation stories recount that the sun god Atun (Re) reposed in the sacred ocean (Nun), whereas the Babylonians believed that the gods (and later all living beings) arose from the fusion of salt water and fresh water. In Genesis I:1–6, the spirit of God is described as stirring above the waters and creating a firmament in the midst of the waters, and in Isaiah 35:4, 6–8 we read, "For in the wilderness shall waters gush out, and streams in the desert. And the parched ground will become marsh and the thirsty land springs of water. . . . And through it will run a path for them which will be called the sacred Way."

Water divinities appear in the mythologies of many past and present cultures, including Greek, Hindu, Celtic, Maori, and Native American. Connected primarily with sacred lakes, rivers, waterfalls, springs, and wells, water itself is often depicted as a living substance that is the primary element on Earth. Although the early Judeo-Christian teachings tended to avoid veneration of natural phenomena, we have numerous examples of sacred bodies of water: The Jordan River, for example, is sacred because Jesus was baptized there. Many New Testament events took place around the Sea of Galilee. The Holy Well of Chartres, the Chalice Well of Glastonbury, and the Holy Grotto at Lourdes are among the most sacred Christian sites.

The term *sacred* is an elusive word that can be defined in a number of ways. According to the *Collins Cobuild English Language Dictionary,* "Something that is *sacred* is believed to be holy and to have a special connection with a god or gods." According to anthropologist James A. Swan, "A thing or a place becomes sacred ultimately to us when it is perceived as somehow able to energize within us those feelings and concepts we associate with the spiritual dimensions of life" (*The Power of Place* [Wheaton, Ill.: Quest Books, 1991]). Native Americans have a related but more expanded meaning. In many indigenous societies, *sacred* means "something special, something out of the ordinary," and often concerns a special part of us because it describes our dreams, our changes and transformations, and our personal way of viewing the world. It also implies something that is shared. This sharing or collective experience is necessary to keep the community's oral traditions and sacred ways alive.

Belief in what is sacred has much to do with our perspective of the world around us. For someone living in a large city or town, the primary sacred place would often be his or her house of worship, like a neighborhood church, synagogue, temple, or mosque. For those living in a desert, the nearest spring or well might be the only place held to be sacred, such as the holy Zamzam well in Saudi Arabia. Yet for the indigenous peoples of the rain forests of Africa and South America or of the Pacific Northwest, the wide variety of plants, animals, and bodies of water may be considered sacred, because they play such an essential role in daily survival. According to a North American Chumash Indian, "I use sacred land every day to exist on. When you have respect for your religion and your tradition, everything around you is sacred."

But just because something is viewed as sacred does not mean that it is never used. Sacred animals—like the bear—were hunted for food and medicine by Native American peoples, and trees like the willow and cottonwood, considered sacred by both the indigenous Ainu of Japan and the Plains Indians of North America, are cut for both utilitarian and ceremonial purposes. Every day anew we depend on water for drinking, eating, washing, watering crops, and many other needs.

One of the main purposes of this book is to remind us of the importance of sacred water in our lives today and throughout the long history of human civilization. We also want to understand sacred water in a larger, planetary context. The Jain religion in India, for example, teaches that because all life is essentially interrelated and interconnected, all living beings— including water—are sacred and deserve to be respected and cherished. By acknowledging the essential role water plays in our evolution and survival, by expressing respect and gratitude, we transform it from a useful object into a sacred subject.

Because we humans are dependent on water for survival, we have maintained a special regard for it since the beginning of time. The sacredness of water has been one of the most important aspects of nearly every world culture since the dawn of civilization. But today, many of us have come to view water as insignificant and dispensable. We have fouled it with sewage, fertilizers, and industrial waste, and we squander millions of gallons of it every day through poor water management, leaky aqueducts, and wasteful personal habits. But water is not an inexhaustible resource. It is not an insignificant commodity that can be used or misused at will. Every well can run dry.

Water becomes sacred when we recognize its powers: as a sustainer of humans, animals, and plants; as a means of transportation; as a vehicle for cleansing, initiation, or gaining wisdom; and as a source of inspiration and enchantment. Water is perhaps humanity's oldest symbol of life, sustenance, abundance, fertility, movement, generosity, permanence, and strength. Sacred water is all around us: from the tiny drops of morning dew on a spider's web to the thundering cascade of a tropical waterfall, in the salty tears that we shed, and in the summer rain that we embrace.

Water is both a common aspect of daily life and an element of rare and inestimable value, leading some to believe that its true worth exceeds that of even gold or diamonds. By reclaiming our inner connection to the sacredness of water, we become inspired to appreciate, honor, and protect the waters of the world.

Nathaniel Altman
January 2002

WATER: ESSENTIAL FOR LIFE

All that the heart desires
can always be summed up by water.
— PAUL CLAUDEL

Water, like air, is a humble but essential substance that permeates every aspect of our lives. Water is the primary ingredient of cytoplasm, which is the fluid medium that makes up our body's cells—cells that also contain a dynamic concoction of DNA, proteins, fatty acids, and hormones. Overall, our bodies consist of more than 85 percent water, which must be replenished constantly throughout the day. A normal adult can survive for weeks without eating, but without water, our metabolism begins to falter in a matter of hours.

Water permeates our entire living environment: Myths and legends often depict water as the blood that runs through an intricate network of veins and arteries of Earth Mother as rivers and streams, providing sustenance to plant and animal life everywhere. In addition to oceans, rivers, lakes, streams, and other obvious natural forms, water is found in liquid form in aquifers, wells, and underground streams; in solid form in glaciers, snow, and icebergs; and as vapor in clouds, mist, fog, and morning dew. Water is also an essential part of soil and all plant and animal life; it is no exaggeration to say that without water, there can be no life on Earth.

WHAT IS WATER?

Although long regarded as one of the Four Elements in nature (along with Earth, Air, and Fire), water is actually a compound whose formula is known to nearly every schoolchild: two atoms of hydrogen welded to one atom of oxygen. Together, they form H_2O, the basic unit of water.

The hydrogen atoms are attached to one side of each oxygen atom, resulting in a water molecule having a positive electrical charge on one side and a negative charge on the other. The hydrogen atoms (which carry a positive electrical charge) attract the negative charge of oxygen atoms that are part of other water molecules, which makes all these molecules clump together.

This is why water takes the form of droplets rather than spreading out as a thin film. The high surface tension of water is also responsible for capillary action, which allows it (and its dissolved substances) to move through the roots of plants as well as through the veins and arteries of the human body.

Water is unique in many ways. It is the only substance found in nature that can be in either solid, liquid, or gaseous form. Water and water vapor exist in continuous movement, allowing them to interact with everything around them. Frozen water is less dense than water in liquid form, which is why ice cubes float in a glass of water or soda.

Water also has a high "specific heat index," which means it can absorb a lot of heat before it gets hot. Water plays an important part in maintaining a constant cellular temperature within our bodies, and thus, a constant body temperature overall. Evaporative cooling (sweating) is another way in which water helps to regulate our body temperature.

Because water absorbs and releases heat slowly, it helps regulate the rate at which air changes temperature in the environment. Communities located near an ocean or large lake experience smaller changes in temperature—both on a daily and seasonal basis—than those located farther inland. For the same reason, water is used as a coolant for motor vehicles and in manufacturing.

Water has been called the universal solvent because it dissolves more substances than any other liquid. This means that wherever water flows, whether through the ground, inside trees and flowers, over the skin, or through our bodies, it carries substances along with it. These substances could be valuable nutrients, like vitamins and minerals, or they can be poisons and impurities, like heavy metals and PCBs. According to Philip Ball in *Life's Matrix: A Biography of Water,*

> Water is life's true and unique medium. Without water, life simply cannot be sustained. It is the fluid that lubricates the workings of the cell, transporting their materials and molecular machinery from one place to another and facilitating the chemical reactions that keep it going. Water is sustenance and cleansing fluid, bearing nutrients to where they are needed and taking away wastes. It is even a structural agent in plants. . . . It enables flowers to hold up their heads to the Sun.

In addition, water is a primary source of energy, the essence of life. Thales of Miletus, a Greek philosopher who lived from 640–546 B.C.E. believed that water was the original substance of the cosmos and the only true element from which all matter was created. His view was echoed some 2,500 years later by the controversial scientist and ecologist Viktor Schauberger (1885–1958), whose numerous inventions sought to generate power, irrigate the land, conserve soil, and control flooding. Yet he was best known for his unorthodox teachings about how understanding nature's subtle energies is essential to human survival. Schauberger challenged the prevailing mechanistic belief that water is merely an inorganic substance precisely because it is able to bestow life on all living things. He wrote: "The Upholder of the Cycles which supports the whole of life, is WATER. In every drop of water dwells a Deity, whom we all serve; there also dwells Life, the Soul of the 'first' substance—Water—whose boundaries and banks are the capillaries that guide it and in which it circulates."

His view that water is a living entity—primarily because it has the unique ability to sustain life—is echoed by countless generations of native peoples around the world, who view the entire Earth as a living being and all that it contains as deserving of acknowledgment, respect, and gratitude. In ancient Pompeii stood a simple fountain that provided water for people and their animals. Above the fountain was a stone carving depicting a cloud and a rain god, reminding whoever drank from the fountain of the water's sacred origin.

THE BODY'S THIRST FOR WATER

In his book *The Coming of the Cosmic Christ*, theologian Matthew Fox recounts the advice of a Native American shaman who suggests that if we wish to learn how to truly appreciate water, we should go without it for four days; some feel that even one day without water would engender a completely new awareness of the vital role it plays in our lives.

Although most of us take water completely for granted, it is essential for all bodily processes, and every cell, tissue, and organ needs it in order to function. Water regulates our temperature, transports nutrients and oxygen to every cell, and is essential for the elimination of toxins.

The human body strives to maintain a perfect water balance. At a normal room temperature of 68 degrees Fahrenheit, a typical adult male should drink at least 1,650 milliliters (app. 7 eight-ounce glasses) of liquid a day, whether as water or other type of liquid beverage; on average he also consumes some 750 ml of water contained in food. The process of oxidation, which involves the breaking down of nutrients by the body, produces an additional 350 ml of water. Totaling 2,750 ml of water, some 1,700 ml is later excreted as urine, 500 ml is lost through perspiration, 400 ml is exhaled, and another 150 ml is contained in feces.

This equilibrium is so precise that we feel thirsty if we are about 1 percent below our normal water balance; at 5 percent, we experience dizziness; at 8 percent, the body's glandular functions begin to shut down. When our water deficit reaches 10 percent, we can no longer walk, and at 12 percent, we are near death. Many of us experience the symptoms of minor dehydration like fatigue, headache, and decreased physical performance on a regular basis because we fail to drink enough; most have been spared the symptoms of severe dehydration like muscle spasms, kidney failure, and delirium.

In order to prevent dehydration, experts suggest that most people should drink 8 to 12 cups of caffeine-free liquid, preferably water, daily. Because caffeine and alcohol lead to dehydration, any serving of such drinks needs to be counterbalanced by an additional 8 to 12 ounces of water. However, when we are exposed to extreme hot or cold, when we do strenuous work, when we have a fever or diarrhea (a special concern for children), or when we eat a high-fiber diet, we need to be especially careful to take in adequate amounts of water. Dehydration contributes to the development of kidney stones, migraine headaches, and mitral valve prolapse.

WATER IN CREATION MYTHS

Because it is so essential to life, water is the primordial element that underlies sacred myths and legends around the world. Anthropologists believe that mythical depictions of water had both real and symbolic meanings. Water has always inspired a sense of awe because it is a natural element that has a multitude of vastly different identities. As architect Charles W. Moore observes, "Water moves through the environment in an endless variety of ways: it rushes turbulently in brooks, falls in drops or mists or sheets of rain, rises from springs in trickles, or bubbles up in pools. Water thunders over falls, rolls onto beaches in waves, crashes against rocks, flurries in blizzards, and condenses in drops of dew."

The ever-changing nature of water has fascinated philosophers for millennia. The Greek philosopher Heraclete commented that one can never "walk through the same river twice" because it is in constant flux. Always in motion, water can never express itself in sturdy form, yet it contributes to the structure of all forms. Even though it is highly unstable in itself, water is necessary for the stability of all life forms. Philosopher Frans Baartmans writes that water is always in the condition of being a "potential" of seeds and hidden powers because it can never go beyond its own mode of existence. As the potential fluid contained in boundless space, water was depicted in early myths as the primary life-principle, or the *fons* and *origo* (fountain and origin) of all life on Earth.

The early Egyptians believed in a primeval watery mass out of which had come the heavens, Earth, and everything that they contained. Ancient Egyptian creation stories recount that the sun god Atun (Re) reposed in the sacred ocean (Nun); the serpent-god Kneph was depicted as encircling a water urn with his head hovering above the waters, which he incubated with

The Nile at Aswan

his breath. It was believed that the Nile was born in this vast watery abyss, along with a heavenly river counterpart that flowed across the sky. Though male, the god Hapi was portrayed as having two breasts—with water from one breast flowing toward the northern Nile, and water from the other breast flowing toward the south.

Throughout ancient Egypt, water was considered to be divine, and sacred beings were believed to inhabit lakes, streams, rivers, and wells. By extension, animals like the hippopotamus and the crocodile were worshipped as deities. Fish in particular were considered the abode of the gods. The religious laws laid down by Egyptian priests, for example, demanded abstention from eating fish entirely.

The Babylonians believed that the gods (and later all living beings) arose from the fusion of salt water and fresh water, the source of which was to be found at the head of the Persian Gulf. Their mythical Cosmic Tree was located close to the ancient city of Eridu, near the mouth of the Euphrates River. It had its roots deep in the watery abyss where Ea, the god of wisdom, dwelt and from where the springs and rivers flowed that fertilized the earth. Like the Egyptians, the Babylonians believed that all waters were inhabited by living beings both real and mystical, and Ea was considered the most important. As King of the Sea, he is sometimes depicted as a fish or as a human sitting on his throne at the bottom of the sea. Addad (or Ramman) was a rain god and the lord of subterranean waters; Nebuchadnezzar regarded him as the "lord of springs and rains," and Hammurabi called upon him to deprive his enemies of both rain and water from springs. Addad was also associated with the destructive aspect of rain, especially when accompanied by thunder or lightning. Other deities were more benign: Queen Innini is a water goddess closely identified with vegetation and growing grain. Ishtar is especially connected with streams and canals, vital to irrigation and agriculture. She is referred to as "daughter of the ocean stream."

One ancient Chinese creation myth recounts that the waters were formed by a cosmic egg that split apart, becoming Yin and Yang, or the male and female forces of nature. The lighter parts of the egg rose upward to become the sky, while the heavier parts fell to become the sea. Out of this egg also sprang a giant named Pangu, who grew so tall that he eventually reached the heavens. After his death, the giant's decomposing body formed mountains, rivers, wind, and sun.

The early Chinese viewed their country as the center of the world, surrounded on all sides by four great seas. At the bottom of the East Sea, into which the Yangtze River empties, the Dragon King was believed to live in the Crystal Palace. More than 500 feet in length, he had the ability to rise to the skies, and was responsible for providing life-giving rains. The Dragon King was served by a tremendous army in the form of fish, shrimp, crabs, and other marine animals.

In Genesis 1:1–6, the spirit of God is described as stirring above the waters: "And God said, 'Let there be a firmament in the midst of the waters, and let it separate the waters from the waters,'" and in Genesis 1:9 we read, "And God said, 'Let the waters under the heavens be gathered together in one place, and let the dry land appear.'" There are also Biblical references to the primordial waters that "were commanded to bring forth living creatures" and to the Tree of Life in Paradise that was fed by four sacred rivers. The water flowing out of Jerusalem described in Zechariah 14:8 symbolizes the outpouring of God's life in the waters beside the temple where Christ proclaimed himself to be a "fount of living waters" (John 7:37).

Muslims have always believed in the sacredness of water, claiming that all the fresh waters on Earth originate from beneath the Dome of the Rock in Jerusalem, one of Islam's holiest shrines. In Muhammad's view, the Nile originated in the Garden of Paradise.

The Dagara people of Burkina Faso and Ghana believe that life began underwater, and that the Earth came to be as the result of the union of water and fire. According to the Dagara shaman Malidoma Patrice Somé, Dagara elders teach that this primal water originally came from the "Other world" and spilled into Earth at a moment when the veil between the two worlds was thinned; and when the original Earth flew close by the Other world. Many African rivers were believed to have originated from divine beings or to have been created by the original birth-flood.

According to a Norse creation myth found in the *Edda*, there was neither heaven nor Earth: There existed only a bottomless deep, Ginungagap, and a world of mist, Niflheim, in which sprang a fountain known as Vergelmer. Twelve rivers flowed from this fountain, and once far enough from their source, they froze into ice. As one icy layer accumulated over another, the great deep filled up over time. The world of light was contained in the world of mist, and the light eventually melted the ice; the vapors rose and formed clouds, from which sprang Ymir, the frost giant.

Eventually a god was born known as Buri, who married a giantess named Bestla. Together they parented Bor, who also married and fathered Odin, Vili, and Ve. Buri and Bestla also slew Ymir, and out of his body formed the Earth, his blood became the seas, his hair the trees, and his bones the mountains. Among the early Norse, the honey dew, the food of the gods, and the bees of Yggdrasil, the Tree of Life, came from the divine waters, the birthplace of the gods.

Water plays a major role in the creation myths of indigenous peoples of the Americas as well. The Shuar, who are native to the western Amazon Basin in Ecuador and Peru, believe that the first Shuar man and woman came forth from a rainbow located just above a sacred waterfall that remains an important Shuar pilgrimage site today. The pool at the foot of this magnificent waterfall is revered as the home of Tsunkqui, a water goddess who rides on the back of a large turtle guarded by crocodiles and anacondas. Out of respect for Tsunkqui, the Shuar are extremely careful not to take any more fish from the water than are needed for their survival, thus ensuring the protection and generosity of the water goddess for future generations.

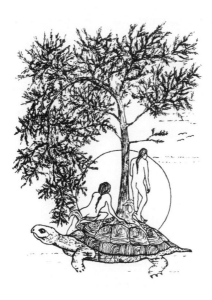

Lenape creation myth

The Lenape, the original inhabitants of what is now New York and New Jersey, share the image of the turtle with the Shuar. One Lenape creation myth describes Earth as resting on a giant turtle swimming in a vast sea. A large tree grew from the soil that covered the turtle's back. The tree eventually gave off two sprouts, which became the first Lenape man and woman.

The *Wallum Olum* is believed to be the oldest historical record of the Lenape people. In depicting the journey of the Lenape to the East Coast from an area near Labrador (discounting anthropological evidence that the Lenape entered North America by crossing a land bridge in the Bering Strait), the document reads:

At the beginning, the sea everywhere covered the earth. Above, extended a swirling cloud, and within it the Great Spirit moved. Primordial, everlasting, invisible, omnipresent—the Great Spirit moved. Bringing forth the sky, the earth, the clouds, the heavens. Bringing forth the day, the night, the stars. Bringing forth all of these to move in harmony.

In Mayan mythology, the surface of the land was completely surrounded by "celestial water" or "watery heaven." Water was seen as the substance on which Earth floats; it is often depicted as welling up out of the portal to the Other world. Among the Nahuatl, also early inhabitants of Mexico, creation was the result of the powerful forces of fire and water, often symbolized by Tlaloc, the God of Rain, who presided over Earthly Paradise, and Huehueteotl, the God of Fire. The Aztec water goddess Chalchiuhtlicue is closely connected to rivers; the mountains are said to be hollow reservoirs of water from which rivers flow. Chalchiuhtlicue is also believed to be responsible for the birth of the first man and woman; a statue on exhibit at the National Museum of Mexico depicts her as a river goddess lying on her back, with a nopal cactus growing out of her body that symbolizes the human heart.

WATER AND THE EVOLUTION OF LIFE

According to Ursula Goodenough, much of the life found on Earth today is the result of several deep-sea hyperthermal events that took place more than 4.5 billion years ago, when water seeped into fissures in Earth's mantle; it heated up and circulated back into the cold oceans. This led to the synthesis of many types of molecules, eventually forming what is popularly called a "primal soup" made of sugars, amino acids, and nucleotides, which formed the basis of all life on Earth. The next step in evolution was single-celled algae and bacteria collectively known as phytoplankton. They are the basis for life in oceans, providing food for a diverse number of animals, including zooplankton and radiolarians, along with flatworms, small jellyfish, crabs, and shrimp.

Today, the oceans make up more than 90 percent of Earth's living space, and the marine life they support is astounding in its diversity, ranging from the blue whale, the world's largest mammal, to the tiny *loriciferan*, a microscopic creature that lives between grains of sand. The Great Barrier Reef off the coast of Australia is home to more than 3,000 species of marine life, and preliminary probing of the deepest recesses of the oceans—where the water temperature is near freezing—has revealed the presence of more than 2,000 species of fish and at least as many invertebrates.

After the first land-based animals left the oceans an estimated 390 million years ago, it was water that sustained them either directly as drinking water, or indirectly in the form of fruits, tubers, nuts, seeds, or other animals. Recent scientific discoveries have revealed the vital importance of the world's coastal ecosystems because it is there that the oceans generate the plankton that provides the base energy for the food chain. Beds of algae and reefs and estuaries are 16 to 18 times more productive than the open sea and provide food for a wide range of fish, shellfish, birds, and turtles. Coastal ecosystems also filter out pollution and function as a natural barrier by preventing land damage inflicted by stormy seas. Many civilizations were founded on the shores of, and sustained by, the oceans, fostering the development of agriculture, navigation, commerce, culture, and religion.

Ocean currents play a pivotal role in regulating the world's climates; without the warm waters of the Gulf Stream, temperate areas like the eastern United States and western Europe would resemble those of the sub-Arctic. The Peru current of South America and the Benguela current of southwest Africa are vital to local fishermen, as they carry a rich harvest of fish. Caused by the phenomenon known as El Niño, altered ocean currents changed established weather patterns dramatically in the late 1990s. In addition to vast alterations in temperatures and winds, El Niño produced tremendous droughts in some regions and powerful floods in others, affecting ocean fishing, crop growth, and regional water supplies.

FROZEN WATER

Water, in the form of glacial ice, created many of the lakes, valleys, rivers, and mountains that we encounter in our world today. The Pleistocene glacial epoch was a period of seven or eight glacial advances that began more than 700,000 years ago. About 25,000 years ago, tremendous glaciers covered some 40 percent of the Earth's land surface—primarily in the northern hemisphere. One, known as the Wisconsin glacier, was an enormous sheet of ice that covered what is now eastern Canada and the United States from Wisconsin to Maine. Scientists believe that the last of the glaciations began to retreat 9,000 years ago in Europe, followed by another 1,000 years later in Canada. Today, only two major ice sheets cover Antarctica and much of Greenland (although they hold less than 6 percent of the world's fresh water, their complete melting would cause the level of the world's oceans to rise approximately 330 feet), in addition to smaller ice caps in the Canadian Arctic, Iceland, and Norway.

Bionnassay Glacier, France

We find mountain glaciers in Alaska and in the Rocky Mountains, as well as in South America, New Zealand, the Himalayas, and Europe. Long-favored by mountain climbers, the majestic Bionnassay in the French Alps remains one of the most visited glaciers in the world today.

Glaciers were responsible for dramatic alterations in the climate, water levels of the oceans, and depressions of Earth's crust and caused tremendous migrations of both plants and animals. In some cases, entire species became extinct when they could not adapt to (or escape) these changes in geography and climate.

California's Yosemite Valley was formed in part by two large glaciers that joined as one and the spectacular erosion activity that followed. The Appalachian, Allegheny, Adirondack, Catskill, and Green Mountains as well as some of the most beautiful bodies of water in North America—including the Great Lakes and the St. Lawrence, Ohio, and Hudson Rivers—owe their existence to glaciers. Although the rivers, mountains, and rocky soil posed major challenges to early human settlers, they also provided abundance in the form of animals for hunting and fishing, forests for fuel, shelter and food, and fertile soil for growing crops.

WATER AND THE POWER OF DEATH

Since our ancestors first began to walk upon the earth, we have harbored ambivalent feelings toward water. On one hand, it was revered as life's essence. On the other, it was perceived as a mysterious and unknown entity capable of tremendous and unrelenting destruction. By its very nature, moving water erodes everything it touches, and violent rains, stormy seas, tidal waves, floods, and raging currents often brought death and destruction to our ancestors, as they still do to us today. In addition to snakes, sharks, and crocodiles, the waters have been the home to a wide variety of dangerous creatures, both mystical and real. As a result, water was often connected to the underworld, a world inhabited by dark and highly dangerous dragons, giants, and man-eating sea serpents.

The almost universal belief in the sacredness of streams, rivers, lakes, and oceans may be due in part to water's natural qualities of movement and sound, and its amazing ability to

Sea serpent

reflect light and offer images of ever-changing living sparks. These qualities not only make the water seem alive, but also inspire the belief that streams, rivers, and springs are the homes of deities. In addition to gods and sea spirits like naiads, a wide variety of fish, as well as turtles, otters, alligators, seals, dolphins, and whales were often regarded as sacred. Particular reverence is given to animals that can live both in water and on land because they are believed to be able to commune with both the heavens and the underworld. Among the indigenous people of what is now the northeastern United States the turtle is a messenger of the spirits and plays a role in healing ceremonies, while the otter, connected to the powers of the underworld, is considered a mighty medicine, and helps its human allies achieve wealth and personal destiny.

Because water is such an excellent solvent, it can carry both life-giving substances like minerals and salts, as well as poisons and other toxins. Most cannot be perceived through our ordinary senses. Such invisible and odorless dangers are another reason why our early human ancestors held water in both awe and fear and sought to respect it as sacred.

The powers of water to bring both life and death were addressed by Viktor Schauberger: Because water in his view was a living entity, it could be both healthy and diseased and even alive and dead. Ahead of his time, he knew that pollution, misuse, and improper handling would make water unhealthy for living beings. He also spoke out against modern methods of irrigation and flood control, as well as the consequences of sterilization and chlorination of water. Schauberger believed that when we fail to perceive water as a living entity which nurtures all life, we run the risk of transmuting it into a dangerous enemy.

The ancient Greeks viewed Earth as both flat and circular and divided into two equal parts by the sea. Around Earth flowed the "River Ocean," providing a steady stream of water. The sea and all the rivers received water from it. In Greek mythology, great rivers and dreaded streams flowed between the world of the living and the dead. The first was Oceanus, the mythical ocean that took the form of a vast sea of nine rings that surrounded Earth. The Styx was the river of Hades, the underworld, and the souls of the dead had to cross it on their journey from the land of the living. Yet the Styx was also

The World according to Homer

regarded as a river of life. When Achilles was born, his mother, Thetis, tried to give him immortality by dipping him into the magic waters of the Styx. But because she forgot to also dip his heel by which she held him, Achilles was left both vulnerable and mortal.

Poseidon, the god of the seas and brother of Zeus, was depicted in Greek mythology as being surrounded by fierce monsters of the deep—some of whom had evolved with the original chaos—as he moved through his watery domain. Sailors feared him greatly because a storm could easily capsize a boat and send its crew to the depths below; thus, offerings to Poseidon would be made to assuage his fury before beginning a voyage. Naval warriors also sought his blessing before undertaking a sea battle. It is believed that Persian galleys captured by the Greeks were dedicated to Poseidon after the great naval victory at Salamis in 480 B.C.E. Because Poseidon was also the god of springs and earthquakes, land-dwellers revered him as well. Horses and bulls were sacred to Poseidon and were sacrificed in his honor, often by being thrown into the sea.

The Tibetans consider lakes and rivers the home of the *lu,* who are frequently depicted as serpent-bodied mermaids and mermasters not unlike the *nagas* of Hindu mythology. According to anthropologist Peter Gold, the lu provide health and prosperity when one attunes one's thoughts, expressions, and actions to them through meditative visualization; however, polluting a stream or lake is believed to provoke disharmony with the resident lu and to bring about illness and misfortune.

It is not uncommon for Tibetans to leave offerings of food, butter, and prayer flags at strategic spots near lakes, rivers, and streams to gain a lu's beneficent blessings.

Native peoples of what is now the United States have held that water spirits (also called water babies) are messengers to the underworld, and thus, should be treated with great respect. Among some cultures, they have traditionally been regarded as benign: Nez Percé children would be expected to offer discarded teeth to water spirits, with the hope of forging a lasting communion with them. The Navajo believe in a being called Water Monster, which looks like an otter but has the horns of a buffalo. Considered a benevolent spirit, Water Monster keeps mountain springs open and the rivers flowing. Another benign deity, known as Water Sprinkler, has the ability to separate and walk through deep or underground waters. As the rain-bringer and water-carrier of the gods, Water Sprinkler produces rain by collecting celestial waters in his jar and sprinkling them in the four directions. He has also been given the duty to extinguish fire.

In most Native American cultures, however, water spirits were considered dangerous and were often depicted in myth and legend as small, solitary beings with long hair who stole unguarded babies at night and pulled unwary people into rivers and lakes. Among the Lakota, the water monsters were seen as creators of floods, which they spewed out of their mouths and who would also catch people and animals and eat them at will. Whenever they needed to ford a river, the Incas would drink the water and pray to the water spirits that they not be grabbed by the current. This ancient custom is connected to a more contemporary ritual in Peru where a newborn baby is given a drink of lukewarm bath water before entering the bath for the first time.

The early Native American views about enchanted water were akin to those of the Celts, who depicted faeries as having the power to enchant humans to enter into their watery realm, where they would kidnap them by drowning. In medieval times, drownings were widely attributed to the seductive power of these faeries who would forever guard the souls of the drowned victims in their watery domain. For this reason, it was considered dangerous to go bathing, especially on feast days held to honor the water faeries. It was also deemed unwise to try to save a person from drowning, lest one may provoke the wrath of a faerie, who may take his or her revenge by causing more drownings later on.

Alaskan myths speak of a deadly sea serpent known as *Amikuk*, who attacked unwary hunters and dragged them from their kayaks into the ocean depths, and the *Aziwugum*, a powerful doglike creature who had the scales of a fish and a lethal tail. Images of water creatures also abound in the lore of groups of the Pacific Northwest. Kwakiutl myths describe the dreaded *Sisiutl*, a huge serpentlike creature with two heads that could swim like a fish, and travel both above and under the ground. It was reputed to kill and eat the flesh of anyone who saw it. Some legends warned that touching its slimy tail or even viewing the Sisiutl would turn people into stone or foam: In some cases, they would vanish altogether. However, those who conquered the Sisiutl would never die, and its protective image could be found adorning house entrances, as well as dance masks and other ceremonial articles.

The ocean and its creatures have always been sources of mystery. While potentially providing a rich bounty, strong currents and storms (and even the animals themselves, as described in *Moby Dick*) made fishing and whaling among the most dangerous endeavors.

Acknowledging both the abundance and fickle temperament of the seas, a festival known as Blessing of the Fleet takes place annually in European and American ports. On the day of the blessing, the fishermen march to their church, sometimes carrying banners emblazoned with the names of their boats. St. Peter and St. Anthony are often the patron saints for this festival: Peter because he was a fisherman himself and Anthony because he stood on the riverbank and preached to the fishes, who rose up on their tails and listened. At the conclusion of the Mass, the entire community forms a procession to the pier for the blessing of the fleet. This often somber ceremony not only asks for divine protection of both the fishermen and their boats, but commemorates those who lost their lives while performing one of the most dangerous jobs in the world.

Inuit igloo

ICE AND SNOW

Among native peoples of North America, ice, just like water, is often allied with death. This may be due to ancestral memories of the Ice Age, which made regions in the northern latitudes uninhabitable and forced these prehistoric groups to undertake difficult and dangerous migrations to more hospitable southern regions.

Many of us have mixed emotions about ice and snow. Whenever it snows, happy children race their sleds down the nearest hill. At the same time, the snow makes roads slippery and treacherous for drivers. Ice storms wreak havoc on power lines and trees. Those of us in colder climates go to tremendous effort to eliminate ice and snow from our lives.

Yet for the Inuit of the Arctic Circle, ice and snow serve as essential sources of fresh water for drinking and cleaning. Ice also supplies building blocks for igloos that provide hunting shelters, house families, and protect their food supplies during much of the year.

THE GREAT FLOOD

The primeval flood is a potent part of human history and myth, and many world cultures, including the Hebrew, Babylonian (the Gilgamesh Epic), Greek, Chinese, and Amerindian, speak of a great deluge that destroyed entire civilizations. Some geologists believe that the floods originated at a time when Earth underwent major climactic and geological changes, over 8,000 years ago. These consisted not only of heavy rains, melting glaciers, tidal waves, and flooding, but also of earthquakes and volcanic eruptions that may have destroyed many human settlements. Taken together, these earth changes led to the formation of mountains, valleys, and islands that remain prominent features of our geographic reality today.

The most famous of these myths is the Biblical story of Noah and the Ark, told in Genesis 6–9. God, being upset at mankind's wickedness, resolved to destroy "man and beast and creeping things and birds of the air." However, Noah was righteous and found favor with God, who ordered him to build an ark out of gopher wood 300 cubits (450 feet) long, 50 cubits (75 feet) wide, and 30 cubits (45 feet) high. Noah did as he was told, and brought his family (eight people in all) and male and female pairs of "animals of every sort" into the ark with enough food to keep them alive. For 40 days and nights it rained, until the highest mountains were covered with water. It took several months before the flood had abated enough for the ark to come to rest on Mount Ararat.

After 40 days, Noah sent out a raven, to no avail. He next sent out a dove, which returned without finding a perch; a week later he sent out the dove again, and it returned with a plucked-off olive leaf in its bill. The following week, the dove did not return. Noah, his family, and the animals emerged from the ark and God promised never again to destroy all living creatures with a flood, giving the rainbow as a sign of this covenant.

The Greek version of the great flood tells of Zeus, who was unhappy with mankind:

> [Zeus], observing the condition of things, burned with anger. He summoned his gods to council. He set forth to the assembly the frightful condition of the earth, and announced the intention to destroy its inhabitants, and providing a new race, unlike the present, which should be worthier of life, and more reverent towards the gods. Fearing lest a conflagration might set Heaven itself on fire, he proceeded to drown the world. Speedily the race of men, and their possessions, were swept away by the deluge.

Stories about the great flood can also be found among most Native American peoples. The following legend is from the Caddo, who lived in what is now Oklahoma:

One time a long, hot, dry season came and all the waters of the earth dried up. The people wandered from place to place, trying to find water, and after many days they became crazed and did many foolish things. While they were acting foolishly they looked up and saw a man in the sky coming toward them from the west. A wind blew, and the man approached and landed on the ground before them. In his hand he carried a small green leaf. He told the people that they had not acted wisely and had abused him, and that he was angry with them. He motioned the leaf in four directions and drops of water fell from it. Soon the waters grew in volume and arose all over the world, even to the treetops, and the highest mountains except one. To this high mountain the man led a few of the people who he chose, and they stayed on the mountain for four days, while the water rose higher and higher. As the waters rose, the man caused the mountain to rise with them; he could do this because he had greater power than the spirit of Cold and Heat. After a time, the waters began to go down, and green things appeared upon the earth again. Then he led the people down from the mountain. They found that many people who had been left in the water during the flood had not drowned, but had turned into alligators and other water animals.

*Chalchiuhtlicue as fish goddess in water descending
to first man and woman, survivors of a deluge* (Codex Vaticanus A)

The Aztec water goddess Chalchiuhtlicue was associated
with a great flood, which was believed to have begun when the
Ancient One judged his creations to be imperfect and that a
deluge was needed to remove them from Earth, with the exception of one male and one female. One ancient codex portrays
her as standing on foaming water covered with sacrificial
images, while a drawing from the *Codex Vaticanus A* portrays
Chalchiuhtlicue as a fish goddess descending toward the first
man and woman, the only survivors of the deluge.

The great flood also resonates in the myths and legends of
the Maori, the original inhabitants of Aotaeroa, now known as
New Zealand. As in other cultures, it was believed that as
humans multiplied, they forgot the laws of righteousness and

became increasingly evil. One Maori myth (which is strikingly similar to that of Noah and the Ark) tells of Parawhenuamea, who was jeered and cursed by his neighbors for his worship of Tane, the progenitor of humanity, the father of trees and birds, the god of light, and the fertilizer of plants. Seeing that all was hopeless, Parawhenuamea and his father built a raft made of two sacred trees and placed fern roots, sweet potatoes, and dogs on deck. The two men then prayed for rain to convince the people of Tane's power, which resulted in a five-day deluge, causing the raft to float away on the Tohinga River and killing everybody left behind. The raft floated for eight months before the waters subsided.

In Chinese myth, the goddess Nu Kua (also known as *Jokwa* in Japan) fought against the giants and demons who were held responsible for the flood, and stopped the rising waters by loading the riverbanks with charred reeds. After the flood had subsided, Nu Kua created an army of powerful dragons to maintain order in the world. Another version tells of Nu Kua saving the world after the four poles holding up the sky had collapsed, leading to tremendous downpours and flooding. Nu Kua is depicted as mending the sky and thus saving the world from extinction. Some believe that the Nu Kua myth also reflects the channeling of unruly waters in order to cultivate land. The legends of Nu Kua are still alive today; reportedly people living near the Yangtze and Yellow rivers still invoke her blessing whenever floods threaten homes and fields.

2

SUSTENANCE

The supreme good is like water, which nourishes all things without trying to.

—LAO TZU

In his *Canticle to the Sun*, Francis of Assisi referred to water as "humble, precious and chaste." As the source of life itself, many of the world's early civilizations—including the Egyptians, Jews, Greeks, Romans, Hindus, Chinese, and Maya—believed that water was a gift of the Divine deserving both reverence and respect. Acknowledging the importance of water for human survival, many early cultures actively protected sources of water such as wells, springs, lakes, and rivers. The Greek historian Herodotus wrote of the Persians: "They neither urinate into rivers nor spit into them,

and they do not wash their hands in them. They do not toler-
ate anyone else from doing so either, and have a very special
respect for rivers." Unfortunately, the ancient Persian respect
for water has not been universally adopted by humanity. Not
only is water often taken for granted—especially when found
in abundance—but also waterways, from the Hudson to the
Yangtze, have frequently been used as convenient sewers, or,
like the Jordan and Euphrates, are excessively drained to provide fresh water for agriculture, industry, and domestic needs.

Many of us today are far removed from our water's natural
sources. Because it travels mostly underground, the water we
use daily is hidden from view; when we turn on the faucet to a
sink or shower, it magically appears, and when we flush a toilet or pull the plug in a sink or bathtub, it disappears forever.
But even though we rarely experience the natural world of
water in our homes and businesses, fresh water is more important to us than ever and provides our primary form of sustenance on many levels.

THE WATER PLANET

Because of its abundance, Earth has rightly been called the
Water Planet. The estimated volume of salt water in the oceans
is approximately 321 million cubic miles, which amounts to
nearly 97 percent of all the water on Earth. By contrast, our
total amount of fresh water is relatively small, and even less of
it is available for human consumption. Three-quarters of

Earth's fresh-water supply is locked in ice caps and glaciers. Although it covers approximately 5.7 percent of Earth's surface, ice contains just 2 percent of its water. However, due to the greenhouse effect, this 2 percent has a crucial influence on our global climate and the environment as the melting polar ice caps raise the sea level.

Underground water (found primarily in aquifers and underground springs) totals 2.526 million cubic miles. Lakes and ponds contain another 427 thousand cubic miles of fresh water, and the flowing water in all of the world's rivers (including water in transit at any given moment) totals 500 cubic miles. Soil moisture contains 32,000 cubic miles, whereas water in the atmosphere (in the form of clouds, ice, and rain) totals only 3,100 cubic miles.

Water is not exclusive to Earth; it has recently been discovered on other planets and may exist in other parts of the universe as well. The *Clementine* spacecraft launched in 1994 found evidence of ice on the Moon, estimated to be 25 feet thick and held within a large crater. Several exploratory spacecraft, including the Mars Global Surveyor spacecraft in 2000, also revealed evidence of outflow channels (believed to have been caused by floods), ancient rivers, and shallow seas on the surface of Mars. Some astronomers speculate that much of the water on Mars is locked up as permanent underground ice, just like in northern Siberia and Canada. Europa, the most explored of Jupiter's moons, is believed to hold more water than all the oceans of Earth combined, containing a vast shell of water and ice that is more than a hundred miles deep.

Despite the relative abundance of usable water (i.e., water exclusive of glaciers and polar ice caps) on our planet, it is not evenly distributed. Brazil, for example, contains approximately one-fifth of all fresh-water resources, but most of it is found in the Amazon basin, where relatively few people live. India, too, has abundant water supplies, but it is not distributed evenly, with some areas of the subcontinent enjoying heavy rainfall and adequate water for drinking and agriculture, whereas arid regions are barely able to support their human and animal populations.

As happens around the world, a large amount of India's valuable water is being polluted by industrial waste and untreated sewage. Two of its most sacred rivers are also its most degraded, the Ganges and the Yamuna, which flows through major cities such as Delhi and Allahabad. In addition to chemical pollution from factories and fertilizer runoff, more than 50 million gallons of untreated sewage flow into the Yamuna every day. Ironically, both rivers are revered as the actual bodies of two of the most important female deities in the vast Hindu pantheon of gods and goddesses and have served as holy pilgrimage sites for literally thousands of years.

Canada and China each contain approximately 5.7 percent of the world's fresh-water supplies. Yet while Canada's population is a mere 30 million people, China must support nearly 50 times as many. One of the major challenges facing humanity is how to conserve water and distribute it more equitably.

WATER: A DAILY BLESSING

Whenever most of us need water for washing or drinking, we simply turn on the tap and it gushes out of the faucet. This is in stark contrast to the developing regions of the world, where an estimated 1 billion people lack clean drinking water and another 3 billion have no access to sanitary services such as bathrooms and showers.

In the United States, domestic water use, including water for drinking, cooking, cleaning, and activities such as washing

Doing laundry, Taxco, Mexico

clothes and dishes, filling the swimming pool, and watering the lawn, averaged 326 gallons a day per household in 1995. Although the amount of water each person uses at home has been declining slightly over the past 20 years, thanks to modern plumbing, water conservation, and metering (which measures water consumption and helps determine municipal usage fees), our growing population is expected to use 45 billion gallons of water per day by 2040, up from 32 billion in 1995.

The average person in a Western industrialized country like the United States utilizes 100 times more water than his or her counterpart in a developing nation such as Cambodia, Honduras, or Uganda. Much of this water is not even used for essential needs like drinking, cooking, or bathing, but for a lush lawn, a shiny car, or a spotless driveway. In addition to individual waste, a large percentage of fresh water destined for municipal use is lost through leaks in the infrastructure. A recent article in the *New York Times* reported that one of the aqueducts supplying water to New York City, known as the Delaware Tunnel, is believed to lose between 10 to 38 million gallons a day, and has been doing so for many years. London loses nearly half of its drinking water because of old, cracked, and leaky pipes.

The ongoing trend of urbanizing desert areas in the United States has increased domestic water consumption dramatically. Cities such as Los Angeles, Albuquerque, Phoenix, Tucson, and Las Vegas rely heavily on imported water supplies, which are often extracted from far-off rivers, lakes, and aquifers and piped to these cities more than hundreds of miles away. In addition to water used to generate electric power (air conditioning is a major consumer of electricity in these naturally hot places), gardens with lush, green lawns and plants not native to the desert and the proliferation of golf courses in naturally arid areas are some of the most wasteful uses of precious water resources in the western states.

WATER AND TREES: THE VITAL LINK

All life is interrelated, and each living entity depends on another for its survival. Like the water that sustains them, trees have always been an integral part of the planetary ecosystem, and life without them would not only be bleak, but also impossible.

Tree in autumn, China

Trees provide much of the oxygen we need to live. One hectare (approximately two-and-one-half acres) of mature forest produces 30 tons of oxygen annually: enough to satisfy the oxygen needs of 300 humans for an entire year. They also absorb many of the chloroflourocarbons (CFCs) that destroy the ozone layer, as well as other particles and gases from the atmosphere, including carbon dioxide, one of the major causes of the greenhouse effect. In addition to providing food and shelter for wildlife, trees shade our homes and businesses, thus reducing the need for fans and air conditioners in the summer months by up to 40 percent. Trees near rivers, lakes, and streams keep water temperatures down, enabling fish to spawn, grow, and thrive. Trees not only fertilize the land, but also prevent soil erosion with their often complex and abundant root systems. By serving as windbreaks in many agricultural areas, trees (such as the Lombardy poplar) help prevent soil loss and crop destruction.

Trees are totally dependent on abundant supplies of water for their growth and well-being, and bodies of water—such as streams, rivers, and aquifers—depend on trees. The roots of trees naturally absorb rainwater, and allow it to gradually release throughout the local bio-region, preserving valuable grasses and topsoil. When people cut down trees—especially through modern clear-cutting techniques—the land is no longer able to retain water, and erosion results. The soil washed from the denuded hills often winds up in rivers and streams, fouling them with silt and increasing the threat of flash floods.

During the past decade, dozens of devastating floods—including those in the American Midwest, northern Italy, England, and northern Venezuela—have been linked to deforestation.

This problem has been compounded by straightening natural river channels and building dams and levees. Although these practices may facilitate shipping and allow people to settle in flood plains, they also destroy native species and increase the potential for flash floods. When high rains occur and a dam or levee is breached, tremendous destruction can occur, as seen in the flooding of the Missouri and Mississippi rivers (and their tributaries) in 1997.

An integral part of the hydrological cycle, the process of transpiration in trees causes water to evaporate into the atmosphere, forming clouds and eventually rain. When forests are destroyed, Earth's surface dries out and reflects more of the sun's heat back into the atmosphere in ways that inhibit normal rainfall. Deforestation can cause radical climactic changes: Rainfall decreases in areas that have lost their tree cover, turning once-fertile lands into barren wastelands.

Deforestation and the resulting scarcity of water is not new to humanity. During Biblical times, extensive pine and cedar forests were cut for timber, pillars, boards, and masts for sailboats. The famous cedars of Lebanon were used for building both Solomon's private palace and his Temple on Mount Moriah in Jerusalem, as described in 2 Chronicles 2:8–9: "Send me also cedar trees, fir trees and algum [another coniferous tree], out of

Lebanon . . . . Even to prepare me timber in abundance: for the house I am about to build shall be wonderful great."

To accomplish these undertakings, according to the Bible, King Solomon sent 30,000 Israelites, 150,000 captive slaves, and more than 3,000 officers to cut down huge expanses of fir and cedar forest over a twenty-year period. Although famous for his wisdom, Solomon had little knowledge of ecology. With the exception of isolated stands of old cedar in remote areas of the country, the forests that carpeted Lebanon in Biblical times have long disappeared.

Systematic deforestation was also common among the Mesopotamians, Mayas, Aztecs, Greeks, and Romans, turning once-fertile regions of our planet into arid and semi-arid terrain. It is believed that the destruction of forests, and the irrevocable disruption of the fresh-water supply essential for drinking and agriculture, contributed to the downfall of these civilizations.

RAIN: MANNA FROM HEAVEN

Many indigenous peoples have long regarded rain as sacred. Rain has the power to transform a parched and dry environment into verdant lushness. In many early societies, the arrival of the first rains of the season was a cause for celebration, as it signaled the beginning of a new cycle of fertility, growth, and abundance, ensuring the continued survival of the community. In early China, symbolic dragons made of wood and covered with paper or cloth would be carried in processions along with banners asking for rain; sometimes a person following the procession would dip a willow branch in water and sprinkle the street with it, and spectators would exclaim, "Here comes the rain!" Perhaps the world's most ancient rain-producing ceremonies, dragon dances, and processions are still celebrated in parts of China today.

Often the rains were considered to nourish the spirit as well as the soil. According to historian John S. Mbiti, certain African societies feel that rain is so closely connected with the Divine that villagers refer to the Supreme Being as "Rain Giver," and would describe rain as "God is falling." In traditional African societies, rainmakers are highly esteemed because they serve as the intermediary between the community and the rain spirits. Rainmaking involves the use of a variety of sacred objects, especially "rain stones," which are said to have fallen from the sky. Rainmakers also ceremonially burn "rain leaves" and other natural objects, so that the smoke is able to "catch" the rain from the heavens and bring it down to Earth. Other rituals use symbolic activities to attract rainfall, including drawing water from sacred wells, sprinkling water on groups of people, and collecting perspiration and spraying it into the air. Mbiti writes: "As it comes from above, so rain links man with the divine. Rain is a deeply religious rhythm, and those who 'deal' in it, transact business of the highest religious calibre. Rain is the manifestation of the eternal, in the here and now. Rainmakers not only solicit physical rain, but symbolize man's contact with the blessings of time and eternity."

For the farming cultures of Mesoamerica, the arrival of the rainy season was a time of deep gratitude to the gods of rain and lightning, who were among the most revered deities of the Maya, Zapotec, and Aztec. For the Tewa living in the semi-arid Rio Grande Basin in central and north-central New Mexico, rain provided sustenance for the people and the game animals—an important food source. Rain was crucial for agriculture, and allowed the Tewa to grow beans, squash, melons, and especially corn, deified in the form of the corn goddess.

Bringers of rain, known as Rain Gods or *Kachinas,* were revered by the Tewa and other Pueblo groups and were considered "Great Ones" or "Great Fathers" by the people. The Tewa made contact with these spirit helpers through the sacred Rain God Drama, also called *Nu hi.* Traditionally scheduled in harmony with the seasons, this sacred ritual involved several days of celebration, culminating with the appearance of masked dancers representing the Cloud Beings.

Invoking heavenly powers to bring rain was also common among early Jews. The Talmud tells of pious men who would pray to God for rain, believing that the Divine would hear their prayers. However, there is the story of Honi, the drawer of circles, who prayed to God for rain but received no response at first. He then drew a magical circle in the dry earth, stood in its center, and declared, "Lord of the Universe; I swear by Thy Great Name that I shall not move hence until Thou hast shown mercy to Thy children." Drops began to fall, but Honi was not satisfied and expressed his disappointment. The rain turned heavier. Honi was still not happy, so the Creator awarded him with a steady downpour of beneficial rain.

Today, many of us have ambivalent feelings toward rain. As children we are taught the little song, "Rain, rain, go away. Come again another day. Little (name) wants to play." Although we depend on it to fill our reservoirs and provide sustenance to trees and gardens, weather forecasters often encourage us to view rainfall or snow in a negative way, often referring to it as bad, while sunny weather is depicted as nice or good. Rather than embrace rain as a blessing, we perceive it as an unpleasant inconvenience at best; and if we live in areas prone to flooding, rain is often seen as a disaster.

Flooding poses a major challenge for many human communities, yet much of the problem is of our own creation. The greenhouse effect, the destruction of the ozone layer, and coastal water pollution have caused alterations in climate that have been linked to extreme weather patterns such as prolonged drought or excessive rainfall. Undamaged ecosystems have a tremendous capacity to hold water, gradually releasing it into the environment. Marshes, for example, not only decrease the rate of rainwater drainage, but they also provide an abundant supply of fresh water to rivers and lakes. In addition, they absorb excess nutrients (including fertilizer runoff and animal waste) washed out of fields and meadows, thus protecting other bodies of water. Drainage pipes, canals, and landfills often destroy swamps and marshes and lead to increased water runoff. Poorly planned housing developments, industrial parks, and shopping centers seal Earth's naturally porous surface with asphalt and concrete, leading to increased rates of water runoff. Finally, many homes and farms have been built in ancient flood plains, making these buildings especially vulnerable to disaster.

SACRED DEW

Like rain, morning dew was considered sacred in many cultures and was revered as one of the mysteries of creation. Caused by the cooling of the ground during the night, atmospheric moisture condenses to form a blanket of droplets on trees and grass. Early Jewish scripture described dew as a true gift from the heavens and a bounty from Yahweh representing fertility, prosperity, and resurrection. Because dew evaporates under the rays of the morning sun, it was a metaphor for speedy departure and disappearance, both precious and elusive. "The spirit of the dew has its dwelling at the ends of the heaven and is connected with the chambers of the rain, and its course is in winter and summer: and the clouds of the mist are connected, and the one passes over the other." (Enoch 60:20)

Greek mythology speaks of Herse, a Dew Goddess, and her sister Pandrosos (All-dewy), two maidens trained in the service of Athena, the Earth Goddess connected to wisdom, lightning, and agriculture. Pandrosos was considered an extension of Athena, and her dewy blanket was associated with the growth of crops. In the age of Homer, it is believed, a tree bough dripping with morning dew was carried in a religious procession in Athens every spring, requesting Athena to provide dew during the heat of summer, thus ensuring abundant harvests. Since Celtic times, a variation of this ceremony endured in England and northern Europe, when boughs dipped in morning dew were carried through villages as part of the yearly agricultural festival known as Whitsuntide, celebrated on the first of May.

WATER-GENERATED ENERGY

Water is both fluid and heavy and was used to power millstones, looms, and saw mills for centuries. Yet it was only after

Falls at the Paper Mill Dam, Saguenay River, Québec

the mid-1800s that people learned how to extract electrical energy from water.

Even though many of today's electrical generating plants are powered by coal, oil, and nuclear energy, there are more than 300 hydroelectric plants in the United States alone, utilizing over 132 billion gallons of flowing water a day. Major ones, such as those at Niagara Falls (New York and Ontario), Hoover Dam (Nevada and Arizona), and Grand Coulee Dam (Washington), provide electrical energy to millions of homes and businesses throughout the country. In addition, nuclear power plants are located on bays or rivers because they require tremendous amounts of water for cooling.

America's manufacturing industries utilize nearly 36 billion gallons of fresh water a day; in addition, manufacturing calls for 3 to 4 times as much electrical energy as domestic use, which means that we consume most of our energy (and much of our water) indirectly through our purchases. Our standard of living in the industrialized nations—large houses with central heating and air conditioning, several cars, many kitchen appliances, and rooms filled with furniture, electronics, and clothes—requires a disproportionate amount of the world's precious natural resources. Packaging and disposable products add significantly to this problem, especially when they are not recycled. Although western Europeans and North Americans make up only 15 percent of the world's population, they consume more than 50 percent of the world's minerals, oil, and water.

Rice paddy, Fengyuen, Taiwan

WATER AND FOOD

When we bite into an apple, we bite into flavorful water. When we squeeze an orange, we squeeze delicious water. An average grapefruit contains 88.4 percent water, an apple on average 84.4 percent. Broccoli is 89 percent water, the water content in corn is 73 percent. Even foods we would consider dry contain water: 35.5 percent in a slice of rye bread, 5.6 percent in peanuts.

The animals and plants we consume are totally dependent on water for life. Fish and shellfish naturally exist in an all-water environment, while cows, pigs, sheep, and fowl need to drink it. Rice, watercress, cranberries, and sea vegetables, such as kelp or seaweed, are grown entirely in watery environments.

Water irrigation to grow food is common throughout the world. It has been utilized in arid climates such as northern Africa, the Middle East, and Mexico for thousands of years. Today, California's Central and Imperial Valleys, eastern Washington, and the Missouri Basin are heavily irrigated. Overall, the amount of water used in irrigation in the United States reached 134.1 billion gallons a day by the year 2000, although more stringent conservation measures are expected to reduce this amount in the coming years.

We need water in the kitchen to cook many of our vegetables; without it, we couldn't prepare potatoes, rice, dried beans, or pasta. We drink it during our meals. And we need water to clean our kitchen and dining areas along with pots, dishes, cooking utensils, and silverware.

Few of us are aware of the amount of water used in raising livestock. A steer, for example, consumes hundreds of pounds of grain a week that required thousands of gallons of water for their cultivation. More than 70 percent of all corn, oats, barley, and grain sorghum crops produced in the United States is fed directly to livestock, along with most of the soybean crop that is not marked for export. In addition, the amount of drinking water used by farm animals is a major drain on our resources.

The typical Western diet includes hundreds of pounds of meat a year, which involves the indirect consumption of hundreds of thousands of gallons of water. In *Proteins: Their Chemistry and Politics,* Dr. Aaron Altschul reports that a plant-based diet requires approximately 300 gallons of water per person per day, while a diet containing meat and other animal products requires approximately 2,500 gallons.

In addition, pollution from animal farms and feedlots greatly affects the quality of our fresh-water supplies. Waste from livestock often percolates directly into the soil or flows into lakes, streams, and rivers. Runoffs carry wastes that are several hundred times more concentrated than raw domestic sewage and form a great threat to both underground and surface water supplies.

SACRED MEALS

Water has always been considered an essential part of our spiritual repasts. One of the earliest references to the sacred quality of a meal can be found in the *Rig-Veda* (IV.29.9) that reads, "By Holy Law long lasting food they bring us," and the early Zoroastrians seem to have mixed juice from the sacred soma plant with bread and water for their communion rituals. Sacred meals of bread and wine were also popular in ancient Greece, and were taken in the festivals of Dionysos (the god of wine), Orpheus (the patron of musicians), Cybele (the mother of the gods), and other deities.

Among the Jews, partaking of the sacred meal is an important element of the Sabbath. To start with, women make a blessing and light candles. This is followed by *Kiddush* (Sanctification), recited by the head of the house while holding a full cup of wine, a symbol of joy and gladness. After a ritual washing of hands, the meal begins. The *seder* is the religious service that includes a festive meal on the first night of Passover that commemorates the exodus from Egypt and the deliverance of the children of Israel from bondage more than 30 centuries ago. Essential to the seder meal are a series of blessings made over the special food and the washing of hands. A number of symbolic ingredients are used, such as wine, bitter herbs, unleavened bread, and a dish of salt water to represent the tears shed by the Hebrews in their misery.

For Christians, the idea of a sacred meal evokes images of the Eucharist, which has its roots in the memorable Passover meal shared by Jesus and his disciples (Matthew 26:17–30), and the miracle of turning water into wine at the wedding at Cana in Galilee, as described in John 2:1–11.

The communal *agape,* or Love Feast (1 Corinthians 2:17–34), was celebrated by early Christians as a meal complementary to the Eucharist itself. Held in private homes, usually with a minister present, it was an occasion for fellowship and a celebration of sympathy, love, and mutual benevolence. Because shared meals have always had a spiritual quality, the founder of Western monasticism, Benedict of Nursia, insisted that all monks take their meals as a group and remain together throughout the entire meal.

Returning from sea-fishing, Japan, 1863

Today, the simple act of inwardly acknowledging what we eat and drink (and how it arrived at the table) can transform any meal into something special. Whether we eat alone or share our meal with others, recognizing the vital connection between water, food, and life allows us to add a sacred dimension to our repast.

3

CIVILIZATION

The fields laugh and the river banks are
overflowed. The gods' offerings descend,
the visage of man is bright, and the
heart of the gods rejoice.
— IN PRAISE OF THE NILE

Water and civilization are inseparable. Oceans, rivers, lakes, and other bodies of water not only nurtured all of the world's early peoples, but also provided them with unique challenges that called for both ingenuity and resourcefulness. The difficulties of crossing a river led to the invention of the early bridge. Flooding brought about the creation of dams and levees, while the need to channel and store water for drinking and agriculture gave birth to the development of water wheels, aqueducts, irrigation systems, and cisterns. The barriers to movement posed by broad rivers and seas caused early humans to build boats and learn the fundamentals of navigation.

Rivers (and their flood plains) laid the foundations for several of the world's most ancient civilizations and continue to nurture them still. The most important include the Yangtze and Yellow Rivers in China, the Tigris and Euphrates in Mesopotamia (today primarily Syria and Iraq), the Indus in what is now modern Pakistan, and the Nile in Egypt. By developing irrigation and water storage technologies, early peoples harnessed the power of these abundant rivers, and made the important transition from subsistence farming to greater agricultural yields, enabling farmers to support others in addition

Flood time on the Nile

to immediate family members. This expanded economy led to the growth of markets, the founding of towns and cities, the opening of trade routes and political alliances, and eventually the birth of complex and sophisticated human societies. As it does today, the way humans utilized precious water supplies in early civilizations has determined prosperity or poverty, abundance or drought.

Humanity has always been highly dependent on water. Among the early Hebrews, it was considered to be so precious that the first item placed before a guest was a bowl of water for washing his feet; it was also a duty to provide drinking water to strangers who passed by one's home. Although some earlier peoples were able to enjoy a continuous supply of water from regular rainfall or by virtue of living near an especially generous well or stream, others were often challenged by a paucity of regular supplies due to periodic drought. In many cases, water created an environment of extremes: While it could be scarce during some months of the year, floods could occur during others. The degree in which a society could utilize water resources wisely, the better the chance they had of survival, as well as increased opportunities for sustained growth and prosperity.

IRRIGATION

Irrigation, which involves channeling the fresh waters of rivers and lakes to nourish crops and animals, was probably first used in Mesopotamia more than 5,000 years ago. It was vital for the development of cultures in Southeast Asia, China, Africa, Egypt, and Mexico and remains important for their modern descendants. Some 230 million hectares of land are presently under irrigation throughout the world, accounting for some 40 percent of the global food harvest. This is approximately double the amount of land that was irrigated in 1950.

The Mesopotamians, who lived in the Tigris and Euphrates river valleys, depended on irrigation for raising grains like wheat, millet, and barley. Excellent architects, they designed and constructed complex water-supply systems consisting of canals, locks, dams, and wells. As a result, the entire region—from Babylon to the Persian Gulf—was rich in gardens, fields, and trees. Some of their methods were very innovative: According to Francis H. Chapelle, well-digging captured water found in the fluvial sediments. The technique consisted of "digging conical holes into the ground, and lining them with stones as the holes deepened. These stones kept the holes from collapsing in on themselves, while allowing water to flow into the wells. The conical shape made it possible both to dig several feet below the water table and to store large quantities of water."

Because the Tigris and the Euphrates were believed to be the children of the ocean or "the great deep," both rivers were intimately connected to Ea, the god of the sea, and revered as "the soul of the land" and the "bestower of blessings," respectively. At the same time, the floods and destruction the rivers produced occasionally were personified by the god Tiamat, known as Tehom in the Old Testament. Today these two great rivers, which originate in the Anatolian Highlands of modern Turkey and flow through Syria and Iraq into the Persian Gulf near the city of Basra, remain life lines to millions, and are aggressively drained throughout their routes. Iraq, for example, removes nearly 85 percent of their waters for drinking, agriculture, and industry.

The competing need for water from a shared river or lake has long been the source of conflict between peoples and nations. The government of Mexico, for example, has often protested the removal of water from the Colorado River for irrigation and power generation by the United States. This water removal not only reduces the Colorado's flow to a trickle by the time it arrives in Mexico, but also the water is so salinated that it can no longer be used for either drinking or irrigation. Draining the Euphrates and Tigris has been the cause of ongoing tension, bringing Turkey and Syria (as well as Syria and Iraq) close to war. Israel and her neighbors continue to struggle over access to the Jordan. Sharing the waters of the Danube for power-generation has plagued the relationship between Hungary and Slovakia, and long-term rivalries between Egypt and her southern neighbors Sudan and Ethiopia over the "ownership" of the Nile are reason for concern. As growing populations compete for scarce water supplies, the potential of "water wars" becomes increasingly likely in the future.

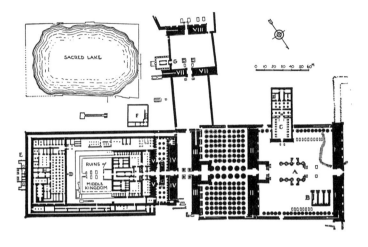

Sacred Lake at Temple of Amon-Re, Karnak

The Nile was crucial for the welfare of ancient Egypt. As mentioned, it was deified and worshipped through the god Hapi, an androgynous being with two breasts, a blue face, green limbs, and a reddish body. Hapi was often depicted as holding two plants, the papyrus and the lotus, or pouring water from two vases representing the abundant waters of the northern and the southern Nile. Many Egyptian temples, including the magnificent temple of Amon-Re at Karnak, featured a sacred lake containing water from the Nile. Here, the lake symbolized Nun, the eternal ocean, and was used by the priests for purification before they carried out temple rituals.

Not too long ago, the waters of the Nile were renowned for their purity. The Canadian scientist J. William Dawson visited Egypt 120 years ago and recorded his impressions of the pristine water: "The waters of the Nile are like those of a mountain stream, pure almost as rain water. Hence their celebrated 'sweetness' in comparison to the more or less brackish waters which issue from springs and wells in the neighbouring desert. . . . No wonder that the fellah loves his river, and that his forefathers made it an object of worship . . . ."

The annual flooding of the Nile has provided Egypt with fertile farm land for more than 5,000 years. Rains in the mountains of Ethiopia wash valuable silt into the river, which flows north to the Mediterranean through a narrow valley flanked by deserts. Until the construction of huge dams in the twentieth century, the Nile flooded its banks and deposited this rich, fertile silt, which enabled farmers to grow two to three crops each year.

During the reign of the Pharaohs, these annual inundations were times for celebration and gratitude; the image of Hapi was carried around in solemn procession and thanks were offered to the god. Other Egyptian deities were venerated as well, including Isis, the virgin mother and the personification of nature, and Anket, who symbolized the waters that enhance the fertility of the fields.

In addition to water for crops, the Nile also provided reeds, rushes, palm fronds, and papyrus stalks for building shelters and boats. Mud from the sacred river was first used raw to build walls; it was later fashioned into bricks, a technology believed to have been introduced from Mesopotamia. The Nile nourished a variety of trees, including the sacred tamarisk,

Boats made of papyrus reeds

palm, acacia, and sycamore. Some, like the date palm, provided food, while the wood of other trees was used primarily for the construction of boats and houses, as well as furniture and religious objects. The sycamore was revered as a Tree of Life, and was dedicated to Hathor, the goddess of fertility, and Nut, the goddess of both the sky and the underworld. Wood from it was often used to make sarcophagi, the decorated coffins that were placed in burial chambers. The river itself was essential for transportation throughout the region; in addition to its role in carrying people and goods from one community to another, the "celestial Nile" was considered a passage for the dead on their final journey to the underworld.

Although the Nile Delta nourished ancient Egypt and her people, the surrounding desert limited the kingdom's growth. At around 3100 B.C.E., the Pharaohs decreed that artificial channels be created to help expand the flood plain. This not only extended the amount of arable land, but also led to the establishment of new settlements. The village of

Fayoum, for example, receives some of its water from the ancient Youssef Canal.

Over the past hundred years, a number of dams have been built to control the flow of the Nile, allowing fields to be irrigated throughout the year as opposed to during flood season alone. One of these was the Aswan Dam, completed in 1933, which was one of the most ambitious dam-building projects of its time. However, the old Aswan pales in size to the gigantic "new" Aswan High Dam, constructed in the 1950s.

Involving huge expenditures of money and natural resources, these dams have indeed controlled the annual floods but have also prevented the deposit of the valuable silt on the fields. As a result, farmers are forced to use increasingly large

Village of Fayoum

Building the old Aswan Dam, 1936

amounts of chemical fertilizers to compensate for the lack of fertile soil, much in contrast to Dawson's description of the silt in 1888: " . . . The Nile mud is not merely clay or flinty sand, but a rich mixture of various minerals, capable of yielding to the roots of plants, alkalis and phosphates and soluble silicates suited to nourish the richest crops."

Large-scale irrigation almost always results in waterlogged land, depletion of the water supply, pollution from chemical fertilizers, and increases in soil salinity levels. Yet if done with care, irrigation can deliver water to fields effectively, as it did in Egypt before the Aswan High Dam began operating.

WATERWORKS

In addition to irrigation, many early cultures flourished by developing ingenious and innovative methods of water transport and storage. Residents of Mesopotamia created a complex infrastructure system including canals, water wheels, public baths, and sanitation. The Phoenicians of Lebanon, Cyprus, and Syria dug water tunnels through solid rock and siphoned water across valleys and hills.

The early Egyptians developed the *shadoof* or wellsweep, which utilizes an upright pole with a cross-arm, from one end of which hangs a bucket for collecting water and irrigating crops. One of humanity's oldest irrigation tools, the shadoof is still widely used in the Nile Delta today. The Muslims of northern Africa invented the *qanat*, a gently sloping tunnel that traps the water of an underground aquifer and channels it to a tank for drinking, washing, and watering gardens. The tunnel structure prevents the water from evaporating under a hot desert sun. Another important Muslim invention was the *noria*, a type of waterwheel that raises water through rotating movement; many early norias can still be found in Syria today. The *foggara*, a variation of the qanat, is an underground system carrying water from many well shafts that converge in canals to supply a multifamily community.

Aqueducts are large manmade channels that carry water from one place to another. The Greeks were among the first to use them; one ancient aqueduct supplied Athens with water until 1929. Aqueducts of different sizes were also used in early

China and Japan, including some that were constructed entirely of bamboo.

In addition to elaborate systems of canals and ditches to drain marshes and meadows in the Tiber River Valley, the Romans were famous for carrying water on tiers and arches. The first was an above-ground aqueduct dating from 312 B.C.E. that supplied the Eternal City. By the fall of the Roman Empire in the fourth and fifth centuries C.E., at least 11 aqueducts were supplying Rome with nearly 90 million gallons of fresh water daily. Aqueducts were seen as the Empire's most glorious architectural achievements, with the longest of them, the Anio Nova, spanning 62 Roman miles, both above and below ground. Aqueducts brought water to Rome for three different uses: It was sent to public fountains for drinking, to thermae for bathing, and to private homes and institutions. Many of these buildings featured "flow-through" bathrooms that flushed wastes into the Tiber. Built throughout the Empire, sections of some aqueducts can still be seen today, the most impressive being those in Segovia, Spain (at 2,400 feet in length, it is characterized by dozens of stately arches), and near Nimes, France, which crosses a valley and reaches a height of 150 feet. More recent aqueducts are essentially copies of those invented by the Romans, as is the one near Querétaro, Mexico, which was built by the Spanish in 1738. Connected to a spring five miles from town, the water made its triumphal entry into Querétaro on 74 arches. Considered an engineering marvel in its time, the aqueduct not only provided the colonial city's

Aqueduct near Querétaro, Mexico

population of 50,000 with fresh, clean drinking water, but it also fed Querétaro's 20 ornamental fountains throughout the year.

During the early Middle Ages, the expanding Christianization of Europe led to the establishment of monasteries as centers of worship, study, and instruction. Many were founded by monks of the Cistercian order, who chose to settle in secluded valleys close to rivers, lakes, and streams: Abbeys like Rievaulx and Fountains in England, Trois Fontaines and Fontenay in France, and Maulbronn in Germany were constructed to take full material and spiritual advantage of local water sources.

The hydraulic wheel, which could be driven by animals or by the force of water alone, led to expanded agricultural opportunities for farmers in North Africa, Spain, and Sicily. Early Muslim engineers built small dams that contained specially designed sluices to allow for the passage of silt, thus avoiding unwanted silt buildup behind the dam and providing farmers with valuable minerals to maintain healthy, fertile soil for their crops.

The growth of cities in the Middle Ages led to the awareness of the need for adequate water supplies for drinking, sanitation, and fire-fighting. By the twelfth century, Paris began receiving water through lead pipes from a reservoir. Siena in Tuscany was fed by no less than six subterranean water systems from nearby springs for drinking, manufacturing, sanitation, and fire control. Some of these conduits were lined with brick and were as wide as three feet across.

In the New World, underground aqueducts have brought water from the Croton Reservoir to New York City since the early 1840s. The water flowed originally into a reservoir located in Central Park that could hold 180 million gallons. Soon realizing that even such a large amount of water would not be adequate for the needs of New York's rapidly growing population, large tracts of land were purchased in upstate New York for a network of reservoirs surrounded by unspoiled forest. Sent downstate through an elaborate system of underground pipelines, these reservoirs continue to supply approximately 1.2 billion gallons of water to New York City a day.

Yet perhaps the most extensive network of aqueducts in the modern world are those providing naturally arid areas of

Central and Southern California with water for agriculture, drinking, sanitation, and manufacturing. This vast system takes water from the Sacramento Delta, the Owens Valley, and the Colorado River and carries it for a distance of up to 550 miles, providing California's Central Valley and the Los Angeles region with 4 million acre feet of water a year. It empties lakes and diverts entire rivers, and even pumps water over a continental divide, thus having a severe impact on the environment. Built and maintained at a cost of many billions of dollars, the Los Angeles basin could not even begin to support its present population of more than 15 million inhabitants without this artificial water supply.

NAVIGATION AND TRADE

When we look at any world map, we find that the vast majority of the world's leading economic, political, and religious centers are located near water: London on the Thames, Paris on the Seine, Rome on the Tiber, and Moscow on the Volga. Shanghai, Hong Kong, Rio de Janeiro, Tokyo, Yokohama, Sydney, Buenos Aires, Cairo, and dozens of other major cities owe both stature and success to their strategic location by water. In North America, nearly all large cities are located on or near rivers, lakes, or oceans. The Aztec precursor to Mexico City, Tenochtitlán, was located on vast Lake Texcoco. Supporting more than 300,000 people and nurturing the religious and political heart of a large and sophisticated civilization, this once-sacred lake has since dried up.

In order to explore distant lands and transport people and goods, early humans around the world developed means of navigation. The first Egyptian boats, for example, were built more than 5,000 years ago from papyrus reeds lashed together. Sea voyages were recorded in hieroglyphics dating back to 3200 B.C.E. Later, fleets of Egyptian boats traveled from the Red Sea toward the Arabian Sea, returning to Thebes with rich cargoes of myrrh, frankincense, ebony, and ivory.

Polynesia was another center of early navigation. Anthropological research has shown that the ancestors of the Polynesians sailed an often treacherous route of more than 1,800 miles from Southeast Asia to remote islands like Fiji, Samoa, and Tonga as early as 1100 B.C.E. Their invention of a double-hulled boat that could reach lengths of over 100 feet made such voyages possible. They also developed outstanding navigational skills that utilized the position of the stars and other celestial bodies, as well as a unique way to understand ocean currents by identifying different types of waves. The early Chinese were equally aware of the environmental conditions of the open sea and devised a complex sailing system that classified no less than two dozen types of seasonal winds, which were measured with weathervanes and kites.

The most advanced seafarers in the ancient Mediterranean were the Phoenicians, who traced their roots to the eastern Mediterranean coast in what is now Lebanon. In addition to being accomplished carpenters and boat builders, the Phoenicians were also legendary traders; their prosperity came primarily from a lucrative commerce in cedar trees, precious metals, and textiles—many of which were colored with a rare purple dye obtained from murex seashells. Along with raw materials and finished goods, the Phoenicians brought culture to many parts of their realm, including the introduction of the written alphabet to the Greeks in around 1100 B.C.E. Eventually, Phoenician settlements were established throughout the Mediterranean and beyond, including Cyprus, Sicily, and Carthage (in what is now Tunisia), as well as Mogador (Morocco), and Cádiz (Spain). There is some evidence that their voyages extended as far as the mouth of the Mondego River in Portugal, and the "Tin Islands" believed to lie either near Brittany or Cornwall.

The Greeks have been sailors and fishermen for thousands of years, and many myths and legends attest to their skill and sense of adventure in overcoming terrible storms, angry gods, and cruel sea monsters like the dreaded fifty-headed Hydra. The fascinating wanderings of Ulysses, in his return from Troy to his own kingdom, Ithaca, were narrated in Homer's *Odyssey*.

In 340 B.C.E., the Greek geographer and astronomer Pythias led a sailing expedition through the Straits of Gibraltar and north along the coasts of France and England to somewhere near the Arctic Circle. Sponsored by Cleopatra, Eudoxus of Cyzicus made several voyages beginning in 146 B.C.E. from Egypt to India in search of spices and precious stones.

Developments in navigation helped spread Christianity across the Roman Empire, as exemplified by the travels of Paul the Apostle. As a preacher, teacher, and founder of churches, Paul journeyed extensively in the eastern Mediterranean, much of it by boat, on three missionary campaigns between 47 and 58 C.E. Paul's first sea voyage began at Antioch, which took him to Cyprus and Attalia. His second missionary journey, which also began at Antioch, took him overland to Troas and by boat to Greece; Paul and his associates returned to the Holy Land by way of Athens, Corinth, and Ephesus, where he is said to have written at least two of his so-called Captivity Epistles to the Ephesians, the Colossians, Philemon, and the Philippians during a period of imprisonment. Paul's third missionary journey (53–58 C.E.) brought him by land and water through much of today's Turkey and Greece. His final trip from Jerusalem to Rome (60–61 C.E.) involved an arduous sea journey to the port of Myra in Lycia and proceeded along the southern coast of Crete and onward to Malta, where he suffered a shipwreck. Paul then traveled to Sicily and the Roman ports of Reggio and Pozzuoli before proceeding overland to Rome, where he was possibly executed during the persecutions by Nero.

FISHING

Several early civilizations considered fish to be sacred. In both the Mediterranean and the Middle East, fish were symbols of life, abundance, and fertility. The Egyptians, who believed fish to be deities associated with Hapi and Osiris, were at times not allowed to partake of their flesh, while the Greeks, who held fish to be related to Aphrodite, ate them in her honor one day a week. The ceremonial burning of fish was an offering to the dead in both ancient Greece and Rome.

Among the early Christians, the fish was a symbol for Christ, and three fish with one head (or three fish intertwined), a symbol of the Holy Trinity. The abundance of loaves and fishes that Jesus offered to the multitudes (John 6:1–15) is said to symbolize the body of the Lord and the hope of salvation for humanity. At least seven of the apostles were fishermen on the Sea of Galilee, probably using nets, hooks, and rods. For Christians, fishing has not only been a symbol of looking into the soul, but also searching *for* souls, as satirically depicted in W. Dendy Sadler's painting.

Thursday *by W. Dendy Sadler*

Based on advances in early navigation, commercial fishing long provided a livelihood for many of the world's peoples. Ocean fishing has been essential for the Japanese, the Portuguese, and the Scandinavians, and fish remains a primary component of their daily diet. Fresh-water fishing has been important for populations who live near rivers and lakes, especially in Asia, North America, and Latin America.

Today, we eat four main groups of marine species. They include fish that live on the bottom of the sea, such as cod, haddock, and sole, and surface-dwellers like halibut, mackerel, tuna, salmon, and anchovy. Crustaceans like lobster and shrimp are very popular as restaurant fare in the United States, while cephalopods, including octopus and squid, are enjoyed in many parts of the world.

Fishing in Lake Patzcuaro, Mexico

Whaling has been practiced for hundreds of years, especially in the United States, Scandinavia, Russia, and Japan. The great whaling days of nineteenth-century New England are long over, but hunting by other countries continues to such an extent as to greatly endanger many of the world's species, including the right, gray, bowhead, and sperm whales. Although the International Whaling Commission (IWC) agreed to stop "factory-ship" whaling in 1979 (which involved large-scale capture and processing that decimated whale populations throughout the world), the hunt for whales on a smaller scale is still carried on.

Humanity's insatiable appetite for fish (along with species that are used as animal feed) has exceeded 75 million tons a year. As the result of more efficient fishing methods and rising world demand, many once-abundant traditional fishing grounds are now almost devoid of fish.

Although strict fishing quotas may help restore some of the marine population, environmentalists call for strategies that acknowledge the fact that one fish species often relies on another for food: Rather than just limiting the harvest of one kind of fish, they study the possibility of a controlled several-species harvest strategy. Equally important is the protection of the oceans and other waters of the world from environmental pollution (see Chapter 10).

Saint Christopher carrying the child Jesus

BRIDGES: FUNCTION AND FORM

In ancient times, fording a river or stream was not an easy task. If a river was deep and its current rapid, crossing on foot or by boat was often a dangerous undertaking, as related by the legend of St. Christopher. A giant of a man, he carried people across a river on his shoulders with the aid of a palm tree as his staff. One day, a small child asked to be taken across. Christopher kindly hoisted him on his shoulders and, staff in hand, began to ford the river. As they progressed into the swift current, the waters began to rise, the winds blew, and the waves roared; at the same time, the tiny child appeared to become heavier, to the point that Christopher feared he would sink under the weight. After an enormous effort of determination and physical strength, Christopher and his passenger finally reached the other shore. Placing the child gently on land, the exhausted giant asked the child's identity, and the boy replied, "Wonder not Christopher, for thou hast not only borne the world, but him who made the world, upon thy shoulders."

In Japan, strong porters used to carry passengers across the flowing waters, as seen in the engraving "Crossing the River to Odawara," dating from 1863. According to Sir Rutherford Alcock, Queen Victoria's "envoy extraordinary and plenipotentiary" to Japan, if a passenger fell into the water and drowned, the porters were duty-bound—at least in theory—to join them in their fate.

Early bridge-building was a major sign of civilization. While respecting the natural flow of what was often a sacred river or stream, a bridge allowed people, along with their animals and

Crossing the river to Odawara

goods, to move unimpeded from one shore to the other. The most primitive early bridges consisted of a simple tree trunk positioned across a stream, a platform of branches laid across two parallel tree trunks, or flat stones or slabs over other rocks in the water. Early suspension-bridge–building techniques were probably used as long as 4,000 years ago by the Indians and Chinese, who also created bridges made with floating pontoons. They invented the cantilever bridge, too, noted for rigid arms extending from both sides of a base that supported a separate central span.

The sixth century B.C.E. was an important time for bridge-building in several cultures: The first bridge across the Euphrates River was built at Babylon; Mandrocles of Samos built the first floating pontoon bridges over the Danube; and the Pons Sublicius was the first bridge to be constructed in Rome. Xerxes devised his famous pontoon bridge involving 600 boats across the Hellespont in 480 B.C.E.

The Romans were master bridge builders. By the second century B.C.E., their engineers had mastered the technique of creating secure midstream foundations and were also responsible for important developments in the design of arches. Some of these foundations were so strong that medieval builders used them to anchor their own bridges. A number of Roman bridges survive today in essentially their original form, including one across the Moselle at Trier and the Ponte Sant'Angelo in Rome, which has proudly spanned the Tiber for nearly 1,900 years.

For early designers, building a bridge presented tremendous challenges. The foundation of the bridge—known as the pier—not only needed to be strong enough to support the arch and its traffic but also had to resist the river's natural flow, especially during periods of flooding. While leaving as small a footprint on the water course as possible, the piers also needed to be secured on a firm foundation of bedrock to prevent them from sinking. The Romans invented the cofferdam, a temporary dam that enabled the dry construction of foundations and piers. According to the *Dictionary of the Middle Ages*, most medieval cofferdams were made by constructing two rows of interlaced piles and filling the empty spaces with clay mortar, making the structure impermeable. Other bridges were built across natural or artificial islands.

Until the development of iron and steel in the late eighteenth century, stone bridges predominated in Europe, although wood remained popular in building smaller structures. One of the most unique bridges, combining several materials and topped with shops, is the famous three-arched Ponte Vecchio in Florence. In Asian countries like China and Japan, bamboo and wood remained the materials of choice through the nineteenth century: The world's longest suspended span (660 feet) made from bamboo was built in Szechuan province in 1776. Many of Japan's wooden bridges were rebuilt as often as four times a century; only one of these, at Iwakumi on Honshu island, survives today. In the United States, many early bridges were simple structures built of wood or stone. Many of the charming

Ponte S. Trinita and Ponte Vecchio, Florence

covered bridges of New England were constructed entirely out of wood. With the advent of mass transportation by the late nineteenth century, bridge-building accelerated tremendously in both Europe and North America, calling for both innovative designs and stronger materials, such as steel girders, spun-steel cable, and reinforced and prestressed concrete.

Bridge design traditionally involves grace and lightness, coupled with strength and elasticity. A bridge serves as a means to overcome barriers and unite diverse geographies. Many bridges—from the primitive structures fashioned from wood and stone, to modern bridges that span enormous distances—are often physically beautiful and deeply inspiring and encourage one to search out new horizons and seek out new adventures. The image of the bridge can be seen as a metaphor for humanity, representing safety and stability, as well as a tool fostering exchange and communication among diverse peoples. Many bridges, including the Peace Bridge between Fort Erie, Ontario, and Buffalo, New York, have served as enduring symbols of friendship between neighbors. Others, like the Brooklyn Bridge and the George Washington Bridge in New York City, and the Golden Gate Bridge in San Francisco, remain beautiful and inspiring structures that testify to the best of humanity's creative vision and engineering accomplishment. (The next chapter will highlight the spiritual dimension of bridges.)

4

SACRED SPACE

The meditative and the intuitive spaces
accessible to human experience are the same;
they are the source of all creativity . . .
— GUNTER NITSCHKE

Architecture has been defined as the art and science of designing structures. Like water, the development of architecture has been pivotal in the creation of human civilization. It not only involves a deep knowledge of mathematics, physics, geography, and economics, but it also calls for understanding the properties of raw materials and how to use them wisely. Sacred architecture, which involves the design and construction of houses of worship, monuments, shrines, and other spiritual structures, is meant to embody and emphasize sacred space. More than focusing on the utilitarian aspects of a building, bridge, or fountain, sacred architecture has traditionally sought to create structures that impress, inspire, and lead to reflection. Its finest examples often convey a great sense of proportion, intellectual complexity, soundness of construction, and harmony with the natural environment. Many have stood the test of time: The great pyramids of Egypt and Mesoamerica, the Parthenon in Athens, the Taj Mahal, and cathedrals such as the Duomo in Milan and Notre Dame in Paris are but a few examples of sacred spaces that still convey tremendous emotional and spiritual power.

WATER AND SACRED ARCHITECTURE

Water has always played a role in the spiritual uplifting of humankind through sacred architecture. In Europe, numerous monasteries and houses of worship were built alongside running water, and often include cloistered fountains, and beautifully carved fonts for ritual purification and baptism. Pools, lakes, fountains, and waterfalls also play an essential role in many sacred gardens around the world, especially in China and Japan. Water is greatly celebrated in the Islamic world, where it has long been a symbol of Paradise in a harsh, desert landscape. Water is available in abundance for ritual washing at mosques—often from beautiful marble fountains. Traditionally hidden from public view behind high walls, Islamic gardens—with their fountains, canals, and reflecting pools—are essentially private spaces designed to provide an escape from the world and invoke quiet contemplation and communion with both nature and the Divine. In describing the Moorish gardens of the Alhambra in Granada, historian Aaron Betsky wrote: "A new Eden surrounds you with trees, bushes and flowers whose presence flows from water. In the entry court, a small burble of water highlights the clean serenity of cool stone pavers."

Wealth, abundance, fertility, and coolness are associated with water in Islamic architecture. Although some structures, such as irrigation canals, were originally valued for their utilitarian function alone, they were later incorporated into the design of elaborate secular and sacred spaces throughout the Middle East. According to André Paccard, "Morocco bestows upon water a privileged place in its cities and homes: irrigation canals in orchards, basins, rectilinear irrigation canals in Andalusian [style] gardens, *mhenshiya* [a serpentine structure for running water] in palaces, marble basins in patios and fountains of mosaic tiles set into walls. . . . Water is ever-present in the life of Morocco and its people continually seek pleasure in it."

Water plays a variety of important roles in sacred architecture that affects us on both emotional and spiritual levels. They include the use of moving water (as expressed through canals, cascades, falls, and chutes), reflecting pools, fountains, bridges, and plants that offer sights, sounds, and aromas that inspire relaxation, reflection, and delight. Among the Chinese, these and other elements have been essential components to the ancient art and science of Feng Shui, a form of environmental awareness concerning nature and how her forms can affect our physical, emotional, and spiritual life.

MOVING WATER

Because the sound of moving water has the ability to calm, inspire, and heal, it has always been important in the design of gardens, monasteries, temples, and other sacred sites in the form of canals, waterfalls, fountains, and pools. Architect Charles Moore suggests that in addition to blocking out unwanted noise, channels of moving water help unify complicated architectural arrangements. In many of the more opulent Islamic palaces, water is actually channeled through marble conduits from room to room, offering the visitor both aesthetic pleasure and soothing coolness. The water may also be collected in small marble fonts from which it descends in the form of rivulets or quiet waterfalls. In describing the Shah Jihan in Delhi's famous Red Fort, historian George Mitchell observes: "There, water is channeled in an open canal that runs through the whole length of the building, in and out of rooms, under screens and platforms, cutting through the floor which it decorates and of which it forms a part. It also unifies the entire layout of the palace, linking all the pavilions in a directional sequence."

Moving water can be channeled in several ways. As a *cascade*, water tumbles over rocks and steps, providing an exciting spectacle of sight and sound. A variation of the cascade is the *catena d'acqua,* in which water descends in the form of channels of different widths. The *chute* allows water to flow unobstructed from one level down to the next. The Islamic *chadar* is a narrow, sloping chute that carries water from one terrace to another, often causing the descending water to reflect full, direct sunlight.

REFLECTING POOLS

Pools offer visitors a sense of repose while introducing a feeling of openness to the garden or courtyard where they are often found. Sheets of tranquil water mirror the patterns of their surrounding elements and raise them to a level that dwells beyond the physical. When located outdoors in an open space, such quiet pools may reflect buildings, trees, or sky, allowing them to appear larger and more expansive; when found indoors, they can enhance the impact of colors and delicate patterns, allowing these forms to appear larger, softer, and more refined. According to George Mitchell, "Pools of water multiply the images they contain, and distort their reality; like the decoration they mirror, they are immutable, yet constantly changing; fluid and dynamic, yet static." One of the most famous reflecting pools in the world can be found at the Taj Mahal, which is considered a structure of singular grace and beauty. Often containing sacred flowers such as the lotus or water lily, the mirror pool elevates an already inspiring

Taj Mahal, Agra

structure to one of great spiritual power and mystery, embracing both the human world and the heavenly realms that lie beyond.

Water not only enhances the image of beautiful structures, but like the alchemist of lore who attempted to change base materials into gold, reflecting water also can transform the appearance of even the most ordinary and undistinguished of forms. As Charles Moore writes, "Reflective water adds an element of fantasy to architecture by filling shadows with light, transforming the solidity of stone or brick to something more transitory and painting what would otherwise be a grey asphalt road with constantly changing color."

WATER PLANTS

Certain plants that thrive in a wet environment play an important role in sacred architecture, and often magnify the spiritual qualities of the water itself. Hindus consider the lotus a symbol of creation, immortality, and rebirth. It is the emblem of the Hindu gods Vishnu (the lotus-naveled) and Brahma (the lotus born), and was connected with the Great Mother Goddess of the Indus Valley as a symbol of fertility, creation, and resurrection. Buddhists view it as the symbol of enlightenment. The Lord Buddha is often depicted as seated on a lotus blossom: The most sacred prayer that a Buddhist can recite includes the phrase *Om mani padme hum* ("The jewel in the heart of the lotus"), a benediction that is constantly repeated on prayer wheels by devout Buddhists throughout Tibet, India, and Nepal.

In Egypt, the lotus was connected to Osiris, the vivifying god of the sun and of the waters of the Nile, and his sister-wife Isis, the virginal Mother Goddess. Mummies often held a lotus flower in their hands as a symbol of resurrection. The blue lotus was especially prized by Egyptian royalty, and was often presented as an offering to the gods. Water lilies were also cherished among the early Egyptians because, like the lotus, they naturally grow in water, which was itself considered a living deity. A symbol of purity and truth, images of the water lily were depicted in many early Egyptian monuments, paintings, and sculptures; the flower itself was often planted in sacred pools in palaces and temples.

The papyrus, or paper reed, from which papyrus is made, was another important water plant, and symbolized the pharaoh's authority over Lower Egypt. Papyrus was harvested for many practical uses, including the manufacturing of boats, fishing rope, cloth, and paper.

Carvings of palm trees decorated Solomon's temple and were used to make booths for feast days. In Psalm 92:12, the palm is a symbol of the righteous. The Gospel of John mentions palm branches that were spread before Jesus as he entered Jerusalem.

In many Moorish gardens, trees that were associated with Paradise—such as the date, fig, orange, and pomegranate—complement pools and fountains to this day. Palm trees provide needed shade for study and quiet conversation.

The willow (whose natural habitat includes the banks of rivers and lakes) has been considered a healing tree and a tree of life among many world cultures, including the Ainu of Hokkaido in Japan, the Celts of Europe, and the Plains Indians of the American Midwest. The cottonwood tree, whose presence reveals a natural water source, was believed to possess both wisdom and healing power by the Tewa of New Mexico, who used the shoots of this sacred tree for making prayer sticks and ceremonial drums. In Asia, stands of bamboo near a pond or stream offer an enduring symbol of constancy and rectitude.

Sizilin Garden, Suzhou, China

BRIDGES: SPIRITUAL PASSAGE

Bridge design and construction were important developments in human civilization, as they enabled people, goods, and ideas to move from one place to another.

In the context of sacred architecture, a bridge often symbolizes a passage from the secular dimension of the known, to an unknown realm offering new perspectives and revelations. In Japan, there are numerous *hachiman* shrines dedicated to different *kami*, or nature spirits. The traditional architecture of these Shinto shrines often includes a sacred bridge or *shinkyo* that spans a pond or body of water. Crossing such a bridge means leaving the secular world behind and entering the spiritual realm of the kami. Associated with peace and harmony, some of the best-known hachiman shrines include the Heian, Washimizu, and Yoshia Jinja shrines in Kyoto, Tsurugaoka shrine in Kamakura, and Usa on the island of Kyushu.

Some of the most beautiful bridges in the world can be found in traditional Chinese gardens, such as the Yudai (Jade Belt) Bridge at the Summer Palace in Beijing. Smaller ones, such as the stone bridge at the Sizilin (Lion) Garden near the city of Suzhou in eastern China, often link the shore to tea-houses and small islands within the garden precinct. Visitors are encouraged to stand atop these bridges and enjoy the view of lotuses and water lilies in the pool below. A fine example of a traditional wooden moon bridge can be found in the renowned Japanese Garden at the Huntington Library in

Bridge in the Japanese Garden, Huntington Library, California

Pasadena, California, where it forms a graceful arch over a tranquil lily pond.

Bridges have also played an important role in religious pilgrimage, including those found on the pilgrimage routes leading to the cathedral of Santiago de Compostela in Galicia, Spain. James (Santiago) the Apostle is said to have fled persecution by the Romans and arrived in northern Spain to preach the gospel. James later returned to Jerusalem, where it is possible that he was martyred in 44 C.E. The shrine is believed to contain his relics, which, according to legend, were miraculously transported from Jerusalem in an unmanned boat to the Galician coast at what is now the port of Padrón.

By the eleventh century, the number of pilgrims making their way from all over Europe to the cathedral at Compostela had grown so large that numerous chapels, monasteries, and guest houses were built along the pilgrimage routes, as well as improved roads and bridges to ease their long and arduous journey. The most popular routes extended from Tours, Vézelay, and Le Puy in northern and central France; they joined with a southern route from Arles and Toulouse at a pilgrimage bridge in Navarra (Spain) known as *Puente la Reina* or "Queen Bridge." Constructed under orders from the wife of King Sancho III the Great (1004–1035 C.E.) with the express purpose of aiding pilgrims on the road to Santiago de Compostela, Puente la Reina to this day crosses the river Arga in a town that now bears its name.

Another famous pilgrimage route, on the Japanese island of Shikoku, leads to 88 temples on a circular route of more than 900 miles. Traditionally, each temple is to be visited in a particular order, with the pilgrimage not considered complete until the pilgrim worshipped at both the first and the eighty-eighth temple. Although the traditional journey on foot can take several months (as described in more detail in Chapter 8), most pilgrims today complete the circuit in a few days by taking a bus, a car, or a motorcycle.

The recent construction of two bridges connecting Shikoku with Honshu brought about a new and unexpected pattern of pilgrimage circulation. Arriving on the Naruto Bridge, pilgrims visit Ry-zen-ji (temple number 1) and then travel counterclockwise to Kubo-ji (temple number 88) before leaving the island via the Seto Bridge. Although a person can never say that he or she has completed the Shikoku pilgrimage by just visiting the first and last temples on the route, this highly abbreviated circuit has been recognized as a distinctive pilgrimage in itself and is called *tobashi henro,* or "skipping [Shikoku] pilgrimage."

Japan is also home to the renowned sacred bridge (shinkyo) that spans the Daiya River near the holy city of Nikko. It marks the legendary spot where Shodo, a much-revered Buddhist priest, crossed the river on the backs of two giant serpents on a pilgrimage during the eighth century C.E.

Wishing to climb a mountain that he believed to be the abode of the gods, Shodo needed to ford the rushing river, but it was so wide and the current so swift he could not get across. Standing beside it, he earnestly recited sacred verses, known as *sutras*. Suddenly, a bearded old man in white clothes appeared on the opposite side of the river and hurled two snakes, one red, the other green, toward the astonished priest. As they tumbled through the air, the snakes grew in size, eventually forming a suspension bridge. Shodo was so afraid of the snakes that he hesitated to cross. A farmer carrying a bundle of tufted grass happened to be passing by, and Shodo explained his problem. The farmer obligingly placed the grass tufts over the snakes so that the nervous monk could walk across.

The original Sacred Bridge was built in 1636 out of wood, but it was washed away by a storm in 1902. Legend has it that

Sacred Bridge (Shinkyo), Nikko, Japan

the bridge was destroyed by a great serpent that swam down the river from the mountains, accompanied by heavenly music and a large number of smaller snakes. The Shinkyo was later rebuilt on more secure concrete supports. An important pilgrimage site in its own right, the bridge is known as the entrance to two shrines and one temple at Nikko.

FOUNTAINS

In contrast to a well, which is fed by its own source, a fountain is fed by moving water, often carried over large distances through aqueducts or pipes. Fountains were originally developed around 4000 B.C.E. in what is now Iran and were used primarily in sacred gardens (our word *Paradise* comes from the Persian term for a walled garden). Based on the belief that the universe was divided into four squares with the wellspring of life in the center, the Persian garden, usually in the form of a square, would be divided into quarters, with four water channels radiating out at ninety-degree angles from the centrally located fountain. This symmetric garden plan eventually became adopted throughout the Islamic world and is often reproduced in traditional carpet motifs. The aim was to re-create the garden of Paradise described in the Qur 'an (Surya XLVII:15):

> This is the similitude of Paradise which the godfearing have been promised: therein are rivers of water unstaling,

rivers of milk unchanging in flavor, and rivers of wine—
a delight to the drinkers, rivers, too, of honey purified;
and therein for them is every fruit, and forgiveness from
their Lord . . . .

Fountains are also commonly found in mosques, where they
are used for ritual washing.

The Western tradition of fountain design is attributed to
the Greeks, whose simple vaselike forms were mainly utilitarian
in nature. Often subordinate to larger architectural structures,
the most elaborate Greek fountains might have featured a styl-
ized animal-headed candelabrum from which issued a small arc
of water. Like sacred springs, Greek fountains were often connected to gods, goddesses, and nymphs. One fountain in
Corinth was associated with the nymph Pirine. According to
legend, when her son was slain by Diana, Pirine cried so much
that she was transformed into a fountain.

Many Greek fountains were part of temples. A fountain in
the temple of Erechtheus at Athens supplied a constant flow
of salt water and was believed to have healing properties;
another saline spring provided water to the temple of Poseidon
Hippias at Mantinea. Some Greek fountains were known for
their magical qualities: One at Cyanae near Lycia was said to
have the power to endow visitors with the ability to experience
whatever vision they imagined.

The simple designs of the Greeks were later improved
upon by the Romans, who were among the world's finest creators of fountain architecture. In addition to providing water

for drinking, washing, and cooking, Roman public fountains were designed to recall the dynamic flow of an abundant spring and symbolized both the emergence and disappearance of fresh water as part of the natural hydrological cycle. According to Charles Moore, "When water bubbles up naturally from a spring, it speaks of the origin, the beginning, or the source of life. At the other end of the cycle, as water seeps into the earth, it evokes the cyclical return and journey back to the source, with images of departure, death, and hoped-for return."

Nicola Salvi, the designer of the eighteenth-century *Fontana di Trevi*, or Trevi Fountain, in Rome, was said to have envisioned the fountain as a powerful affirmation of the water cycle by using mythological symbols of tritons and sea nymphs above the cascading, splashing, and churning water. Located at the termination of an ancient aqueduct known as *Acqua Virgo*, Trevi is celebrated both for the purity of its water and the many popular superstitions concerning the fountain itself.

Along with rivers and springs, the Celts worshipped fountains, and believed them to be the home of deities who imbued them with miraculous powers of healing, prophesy, and good fortune. Christian missionaries could not easily overcome such strongly held beliefs, so they often associated the ancient fountains with the Virgin and various saints. Sometimes chapels or churches were built above the ancient fountains, but usually a statue of the Virgin or a saint placed by the fountain would suffice.

In medieval Europe, the cloisters of most monasteries were surrounded by colonnaded walks and had a well or simple fountain at the center—possibly inspired by Persian or Muslim gardens and intended to enhance meditation and personal reflection. Some, such as the fountains at the abbeys in Limoges, France, and Maulbronn, Germany, are still in operation 600 years later.

As mentioned earlier, the Cistercians had a great appreciation for water and often established their monasteries next to rivers and streams. Many of them—including those at Le Thoronet, Fossanova, Alcobaca, and Heiligenkreuz—contained special fountain pavilions in which the monks would wash their hands before meals. Located in front of the refectory, or dining hall, and hexagonal or square in shape, they were decorated with graceful pillars and arches, and often resembled medieval chapels. In the middle of the pavilion stood the fountain that supplied a continual stream of water that flowed into a stone basin. The basins themselves were often designed and executed with the greatest of care. Other Cistercian monasteries would have a simple fountain and basin attached to the outside wall of the refectory.

Although rarely as imposing as the early Roman designs, most medieval European towns had at least a few public fountains, which often became the social centers of the entire community. In many cases, markets, shops, government buildings, and churches were built nearby, forming the core of lively neighborhoods.

The sounds of water emanating from a fountain are not unlike those from a natural waterfall and can energize, soothe, and heighten spiritual awareness. Depending on the velocity, amount, and direction of flow, water expresses itself with varying levels of volume and pitch—the combination of several types of moving water has the power to create a harmonious symphony of living sounds. It should be no surprise that composers and poets have been deeply inspired by fountains. It is said that while Franz Liszt was living at Villa d'Este, near Rome, the harmonious sounds from the hundreds of small and large jets, spouts, and fountains led him to compose *Les Jeaux à la Villa d'Este* and other works.

THE WATER ELEMENT IN FENG SHUI

The early Chinese were very conscious of the ways water affects human environments. *Feng Shui* (from the Chinese terms meaning "wind" and "water") is an ancient tradition of geomancy and design grounded in a deep sensitivity to nature, which is believed to be the source of *chi*, or vital force. Feng Shui teaches that by learning about the influence of environmental factors such as trees, land contours, and water, we can help shape our destiny. Thus, Feng Shui is widely used to improve health, create prosperity, restore domestic harmony, and improve careers. By being aware of topography, vegetation, site and floor plans, furniture placement, colors and other factors, practitioners of Feng Shui believe that we can radically transform our life and its potential.

First used to help find a propitious location for family

burials, it was originally believed that positive Feng Shui was derived from the presence of the dragon—a protecting force—who resided in rock formations and water courses. According to anthropologist Martin Yang, the dragon is represented by the brink of the stream flowing around a grave; if the burial place is surrounded by water courses and hills (the dragon's natural abode), the departed ancestors will draw power from the site and bestow prosperity, fecundity, and good fortune on their descendants.

While Feng Shui continues to determine locations of family graves, it also plays a major role in the placement of Buddhist and Shinto temples and other religious structures: For example, the ideal location for a temple calls for a hill or mountain in the background (many contemporary temples in Taiwan are built into hillsides and mountainsides), with the front of the temple facing a body of water. The beautiful Kuan Yin Monastery in upstate New York is set into a hillside and overlooks a small lake, while the Hakone Shrine is built on a mountain slope that offers a splendid view of Lake Ashi, one of the most sacred lakes in Japan. In order to reach the temple itself, a visitor must climb several very long flights of steps lined with dozens of ancient cedar trees.

Water plays an especially important role in Feng Shui because wells, rivers, streams, lakes, and ponds are considered potentially good conductors of chi. Water that flows slowly and meanders through the countryside in graceful curves is considered to both conserve and properly direct the

Sacred well, Arima Onsen, Japan

natural powers of chi throughout the environment, while fast-moving water flowing in a straight line (or forced to travel around sharp bends) can allow chi to dissipate and even cause harm.

Still water, be it in a lake, pool, or well, represents wisdom, clarity, and good judgment and has an almost magical ability to both calm the emotions and revive the spirit. No traditional Chinese garden is without a lake or a pool; this body of water, no matter how small, is the garden's spiritual heart. According to writer Yang Hung-hsien, "Nothing else produces quite the same serene effect as a pool where the visitor stands alone in opposition to space and is divinely delighted with its pure expanse." In ancient China, a vast pool was believed to be a powerful source of positive chi, especially if it contained fish, a traditional symbol of prosperity and good fortune.

Flowing water, such as that of a waterfall or stream, soothes the emotions and facilitates the discovery of new ideas. Traditionally, moving water also represents increased energy and personal prosperity: Adding flowing water to a pond in the form of a waterfall or fountain is believed to greatly enhance the flow of chi.

In Feng Shui, water is also the element of communication, thus facilitating the exchange of ideas through art, music, and literature. Historically, Chinese gardens were private retreats where families would engage in scholarly and artistic pursuits, with a tranquil pond or lake often forming the backdrop for poetry readings, discussions of Confucian philosophy, and intimate concerts.

These gardens were originally intended to replicate the beauty of the countryside. For example, the classic pond, common in almost all Chinese gardens, evolved from the fact that water is a vital element in human life, whereas the rock garden evoked the image of the beloved mountains that are the subject of many ancient Chinese poems and paintings. According to the English historian H. N. Wethered, "The people divert streams through their gardens, creating miniature waterfalls, and excavate soil for artificial pools to invite the spirits of the wind, the air and the water. . . . Mountains in the Chinese mind also attract a peculiar reverence as exerting

a propitious influence on human life: the mountains in a garden, if only the size of molehills, have a symbolic meaning
pointing to good fortune."

Chinese philosophy teaches that rivers and streams are the
arteries of Earth and that mountains form her skeleton. As
symbolic mountains, sturdy stones and rocks in the garden
offer a delightful counterpoint to the flowing water, offering
the masculine yang to the water's feminine yin.

SACRED SPACES, SACRED WATER

Water is an essential part of some of the world's most sacred
spaces. Four such sites will be highlighted on the following
pages: two in India and two in England, as well as two peaceful water places in California.

The Golden Lotus Tank in Madurai

The city of Madurai in Southern India is considered the heart
of Tamil culture. Nourished by the waters of the sacred Vaigai
River, Madurai is home to one of India's largest and most
spectacular temple complexes, dedicated to the fish-eyed
Goddess Meenakshi and Lord Sundareshwara (Shiva) and built
mostly between the sixteenth and eighteenth centuries C.E. Any
day of the week, thousands of people pass through its gate; the
number increases on Fridays, which is sacred to Meenakshi.
Towering temples with myriad shrines, sculptures, and colon-

The Golden Lotus Tank, Madurai

nades are framed by the sacred Potramarai Kulum, also known
as the Golden Lotus Tank. According to Hindu tradition, Lord
Indra (one of the Eight Great Devas and the Lord of the
Rains) bathed in this tank to achieve spiritual purification. He
also worshipped Lord Shiva (one of the holy Hindu trinity of
gods, Shiva is known as both the destroyer and the regenerator)
by plucking golden lotus flowers that grew in the tank. Steps
lead down to the water from the surrounding colonnades, and
in the center stands a brass lamp column.

Predating the temples, the Golden Lotus Tank remains an
important Hindu pilgrimage site, and devotees still bathe in its
sacred waters today. Every Friday, golden idols depicting
Meenakshi and Sundareshwara are placed on a ceremonial

swing located on the western side of the pool, and hymns are sung to the deities as the idols are gently swung to and fro.

The Golden Temple of Amritsar

The Sri Hari Mandir, better known as The Golden Temple in the city of Amritsar (Punjab), is the spiritual center of the Sikh faith. Rising from the middle of a rectangular artificial lake (known as Amrit Sovar, or the Pool of the Nectar of Immortality), the temple has been highly sacred to the Sikhs ever since it was built in the late sixteenth century C.E. Considered one of the most beautiful temples in all of India, one enthusiastic European visitor described it in 1898: "In the middle of the lake, reflected in its glassy surface, is the Golden Temple shining in the sunlight like some powerful jeweled casket."

The Golden Temple, Amritsar

The site of the Sri Hari Mandir is shrouded in myth and legend. Some trace its origin to the time of the Vedas as an ancient healing spring known as Amrit Kund (Spring of Nectar). It is said that in the mid-sixteenth century C.E. Guru Amar Das (the third Guru of the Sikhs) found a rare medicinal herb on the banks of the spring and used it to treat Guru Angad (the second Guru), who was suffering from a skin disease.

Another legend also highlights the medicinal properties of the waters: Rajni, the daughter of a revenue collector, brought her husband there because he was suffering from leprosy. After only one dip in the healing spring, his condition was completely cured. The fourth Guru, Ram Das (who was visiting nearby) came to the waters to investigate the miraculous cure. He was so impressed with the beauty of the spring and its surroundings that he decided to make it a center of pilgrimage. The sacred waters continue to be renowned for their miraculous healing powers and are used for ritual bathing by Sikh devotees and especially by the sick, who hope to be cured by swimming in the lake.

Wells Cathedral

Wells is England's smallest cathedral city. Springs of clear water—40 gallons every second—well up to the surface near the cathedral, hence the city's name. The precursor to the present cathedral was built in 705 C.E. by Ina, king of Wessex, who selected a site next to the springs where pagan Celts had previously worshipped the goddess of the healing waters. In the marketplace stands a fountain that symbolizes the holy well, which drew thousands of pilgrims every year during medieval times in search of healing and spiritual nourishment. Today, spiritual travelers come to Wells to find an almost unchanged sacred landscape of cathedral, monastery buildings, bishop's palace, city, and countryside, woven together into perfection.

Fountains Abbey

It is said that early Cistercian monks had much in common with the Celts, who believed in the sacredness of nature, including bodies of water such as springs, rivers, and lakes. This may be one reason why many early Cistercian monasteries were founded in remote, heavily wooded valleys near a river or stream, and provided spiritual communion through the medium of nature, as well as prayer and hard labor. One of the most beautiful was Fountains Abbey in Yorkshire, a great reminder of medieval monastic life. The abbey, today a romantic ruin, was named for the springs of water that gush from the banks above the River Skell, where a party of twelve monks first took shelter under a large elm tree during the winter of 1132.

Near the abbey is Robin Hood's Well, which takes its name from a legendary encounter between two mythical figures: Robin Hood, who was said to have enjoyed poaching deer in the abbey's forests, and Friar Tuck, a man of considerable physical strength who allegedly was the local gamekeeper. Medieval tales recount the long battle between the two men that involved both mental wit and physical prowess, until the friar eventually decided to join Robin Hood and his merry men.

American Water Temples

Although they would not be considered traditional sacred sites, water temples are neo-classical structures connected to modern aqueducts and were built to celebrate the water element in monumental form. Two of the best known water temples in the United States can be found near San Francisco and offer visitors a unique place for inspiration and relaxation.

The *Sunol Water Temple* is located in Contra Costa County, about 30 miles east of San Francisco at the head of Niles canyon. Designed in the Greek Revival style in 1910 by architect Willis Polk and owned by the City of San Francisco, its classic beauty ranks with that of City Hall and the Palace of Fine Arts downtown. Recently renovated and newly opened to the public, the interior of the temple has been called a sparkling celebration of the power of water.

The *Pulgas Water Temple* is another Greek Revival masterpiece in San Mateo County, approximately 20 miles south of the city. Also built in the early twentieth century, the temple marks the end of the Hetch-Hetchy aqueduct. Water flows from Yosemite National Park, passes through the temple, and continues along an open canal to the Crystal Springs Reservoir. Before a protective grate was recently installed inside the temple, a popular rite of passage for local youths was to jump into the water, swim with the fast current through a 50-foot long submerged tunnel, and finally surface in the open canal. Today, the Pulgas Water Temple attracts a quieter crowd that enjoys its parklike setting for reading, picnicking, and contemplation.

5

CLEANSING

I will sprinkle clean water upon you,
and you shall be clean from all
your uncleannesses . . . .
—EZEKIEL 36:25

Water has been called the universal solvent because it dissolves more substances than any other liquid. This means that wherever water flows, be it through the ground, inside trees and flowers, over the skin, or through our bodies, it carries substances along with it. These can be either valuable nutrients, such as vitamins and minerals or poisons and impurities. In addition, water, whether as liquid or steam, is naturally in continuous movement, which allows it to constantly interact with everything around. It is hard to imagine what life would be like without the cleansing properties of water; yet when we wash our hands, brush our teeth, take a bath or shower, clean the dishes, or do the laundry, most of us take water and its amazing cleansing abilities completely for granted.

THE SELF-CLEANSING POWERS OF WATER

In nature, water is a powerful cleanser and purifier. Oceans, as well as rivers and lakes (when allowed to express their natural movements), have the capacity to cleanse themselves of pollutants and other impurities.

Three well-known North American bodies of water illustrate nature's amazing cleansing abilities. After more than a century of pollution from industrial waste, untreated municipal sewage, agricultural runoff (primarily chemical fertilizer and animal waste), and phosphates from laundry detergents, Lake Erie was considered a dying sinkhole by 1969, and was given the ominous rating as one of the most polluted lakes in North America.

This rating eventually caused the area's regional and local governments, manufacturers, and farmers to change the way they view Lake Erie—from that of a gigantic sewer to a living body of water that is crucial to the survival of the entire bio-region. Thanks to the elimination of pollution from factories, reformulation of detergents, improved municipal sewage treatment, and improved agricultural drainage, Lake Erie experienced a steady recovery: No longer regarded as a polluted backwater and garbage dump, the lake is once again attracting millions of visitors annually, who flock to its waters for swimming, boating, and fishing.

Five hundred miles away in New York City, Albert Appleton, former Commissioner of Environmental Protection, aroused controversy in 1993 by lobbying against the construction of expensive water treatment facilities in Jamaica Bay, arguing that ecosystems are designed by nature to be self-cleansing and self-renewing. His unorthodox but persistent approach led the city government to shift its focus from cleaning up the bay with water treatment plants to rebuilding the bay's natural wetlands by working to restore their historic depth contours. As a result, the natural water ecosystem was able to do much of the environmental cleanup for free. New York City was able to reduce the cost of meeting clean-water goals for Jamaica Bay from $2.3 billion to $1.2 billion and created a popular boating and fishing area in the process.

Similarly, the magnificent Hudson River, which flows from the Adirondack Mountains north of Albany to the Atlantic Ocean near New York City, has only recently been able to recover from more than two centuries of severe pollution due to untreated municipal sewage and chemical dumping from mills and other manufacturing plants along its 315-mile length. Known for its diverse ecology and for providing a wide range of resources to a varied constituency, the Hudson was once described by ecologist Robert H. Boyle as "a trout stream and an estuary, water supply and sewer, ship channel and shad river, playground and chamber pot." The river historically abounded with millions of fish, including sea sturgeon, bluefish, white perch, yellow perch, shad, herring, catfish, and carp; but by 1970, parts of the Hudson had become so polluted that it was unable to support most aquatic life. As a result, the river was avoided by swimmers, boaters, and fishermen, and many of the cities and towns located by its shores, such as Yonkers, Peekskill, Beacon, and Poughkeepsie, began losing population and witnessed a sharp decline in property values. Yet, thanks to the sustained efforts of local activists since the early 1970s— led by singer Pete Seeger and the crew of the educational sailboat *Clearwater*—the government began to establish and enforce strict environmental regulations. As a result, water pollution has abated considerably, especially from chemical dumping and municipal sewage. Although it still has a long way to go toward achieving its original pristine aquatic environment, the river is slowly cleansing itself of existing pollutants. Not only are the shad and sturgeon returning to its abundant tidal waters, but the Hudson is also regaining its reputation as one of the most beautiful rivers in the world.

CLEANSING THE HUMAN BODY

Similarly, water is essential for cleansing our bodies from waste and impurities. This constant movement of water, which is regulated by the posterior pituitary gland, collects impurities throughout the body (which consists of more than 85 percent water) that are eventually passed through the kidneys and into the colon and bladder for elimination.

Cleansing treatments involving what is known as the drinking cure are common at many of Europe's leading spas, including San Pellegrino in Italy, Baden-Baden in Germany, Karlovy Vary (Carlsbad) in the Czech Republic, and Vichy and Vittel in France. There patients consume prescribed amounts of mineralized spring water, often directly from the source. Hot springs bathing, steam baths, and saunas often complement the drinking cure. In addition to providing improved hydration, minerals and trace elements in the water that are vital for normal bodily functions and the metabolism are absorbed by the gastrointestinal tract and promote self-cleansing.

In India, some yogis take water cleansing to a level that Westerners may consider extreme. One method involves a daily nasal wash consisting of pouring warm salt water into one nostril with a specially designed pitcher, and allowing it to run out through the other nostril. This procedure is then reversed, and water is forcefully expelled through the original nostril once again. In some Indian villages, yogis drink a large pitcher of water upon arising in the morning; this produces vomiting and brings up mucous (which drains into the stomach from the nasal passages, sinuses, and bronchi) and other substances that accumulate in the stomach during the night. Even more unusual are reports of yogis who squat in a river or lake and draw water into their bladder and intestines through the anus without the aid of artificial devices or instruments. Through what must be an amazing degree of muscle control, the yogis are able to churn the water inside their organs before expelling it, thus effectively cleansing the bowel and urinary tract.

For many, cleansing the outside of the body is one of our most habitual (and enjoyable) activities. A morning shower before breakfast, a soothing bath after work, or even the simple washing of hands before and after meals enable us to feel cleaner and more relaxed and refreshed. In a world where many of us have almost continuous contact with dirt, dust, germs, and other bacteria, periodic hand washing has been found to be an important part of maintaining good health. In countries such as Japan, personal cleanliness is considered an important societal virtue, and in India, even the poorest citizens take a daily sponge bath or shower, sometimes in the street or at a public bathhouse.

THE ROMAN BATH

The Romans could be obsessed with cleanliness, but also enjoyed the baths for their luxury and sensuality. Throughout the Empire, baths such as *Aquae Sulis* (today's Bath) in England, Carleon in Wales, or *Civitas Aquae Aureliae* (Baden-Baden in Germany) were considered the highest expression of bathing culture, and any city worthy of its status would have possessed at least one public bath. The larger baths possessed a variety of

Aquae Sulis *(today's Bath) in England,* 43 *C.E.*

rooms, including the dressing area, cold water pools (the *frigidar-ium*), warm water pools (the *tepidarium*), and hot water baths (the *calderium*), a hot, dry area for sweating (the *laconicum*), and a swim-ming pool, known as the *natatio.* When natural hot springs were unavailable, water was heated with braziers or through heat ducts or underfloor heating. The more luxurious baths also contained libraries, private bathing suites, gymnasiums, and gardens. Some were classified as *thermae,* which were important gathering places for friendly discussion, making business deals, and enjoying the entertainment of singers, dancers, and jugglers.

In addition to being considered vital for health and well-being, Roman baths ranked as important centers of social activity and were especially popular with writers, artists, and politicians.

One of the first public baths in Rome was constructed by Marcus Agrippa around 20 B.C.E., and included both sulfur water and natural sea water. At the height of the Roman Empire, more than 900 public baths could be found in Rome, along with 11 imperial *thermae.* The most impressive, however, were the legendary Baths of Caracalla, described in *A Dictionary of the Roman Empire:* "There were libraries, gardens, gymnasiums and cisterns. The *natatio* was large and positioned to maximize the sky overhead: further, screens and walls semi-enclosed its area. Vaster in size was the *frigidarium,* which was supported by cross vaults and surrounded by small pools. The *calderium* was moved away from the interior of the baths and set in its own position with a magnificent dome, some 35 meters high."

Caracalla also contained a temple at each end: One was dedicated to Apollo and the other to Aesculapius, the deity responsible for nourishing the body. The buildings were surrounded by vast gardens and numerous fountains, as well as beautiful sculptures and quiet, tree-lined promenades.

Many Roman baths were dedicated to goddesses such as Artemis, Venus, and Thermae. Because of their pagan associations and the fact that Roman baths were often popular gathering places for eating, drinking, sexual activity, and other forms of enjoyment, they were not looked upon kindly by early Christians, who considered cleanliness an indulgence and not washing a spiritual act of self-denial. As the Empire gradually declined, many public baths were closed and eventually disintegrated from lack of use.

SPIRITUAL CLEANSING

Ritual bathing, also known as *ablution,* involves the act of washing in order to correct a condition of physical or spiritual impurity and restore it to purity once again. Ablutions can involve the washing of hands, face, mouth, or other body parts, or can involve immersing the entire body in a lake, river, or ritual bath. Some religious teachers maintain that ablution should not be confused with cleanliness; in some Hebrew rituals, for example, the body must already be clean before ablution takes place. Ritual cleansing has been exercised throughout human history. It had been used in ancient Egypt and Greece, and is practiced in many religious traditions, including Jewish,

Monks bathing (during the Middle Ages)

Christian, Muslim, Hindu, Shinto, and Zoroastrian, as well as by many indigenous groups in Africa, Asia, and the Americas.

Before the advent of the germ theory, illnesses were universally believed to be caused by evil spirits, often infecting people who had broken societal taboos or who were undergoing major periods of transition in their lives. Purification rituals involving fire and smoke; physical or psychological purgation, including activities such as fasting or confession; cleansing substances such as herbs and salt; and the use of scapegoats have been used in many religious traditions to eliminate the threat of evil influences and restore wholeness and purity to both the individual and the entire community.

The powerful cleansing properties of water led many religions to consider it the primary ingredient for purification rituals. Water was not only seen as crucial for washing away one's sins and purging evil influences but was also used to cleanse the individual from natural impurities due to contact with blood, excreta, vomit, and cooked foods, which were often considered taboo by society. An important part of these rites involved spiritual protection during major periods of life transition such as birth, puberty, and marriage, when humans were believed to be most vulnerable to attack by negative energies and evil spirits.

The goals of ritual cleansing are manifold, and involve more than just the spiritual side of our nature. If approached in full consciousness, with an open mind and proper attitude, ritual cleansing can encompass many aspects of our being.

Cleansing

Physical purification takes place by transforming the living forces within our bodies so that we become attuned to higher, more refined energies. This process also can inspire us to take better care of our physical bodies through a healthy diet, exercise, and the environments in which we place ourselves, along with proper rest, relaxation, and stress management.

Emotional purification enhances consciousness, thus bringing us toward a deeper awareness of our emotional lives, including the motivations that influence desires and outer behavior. It leads us to be more aware of the choices we make in life and what lies behind them.

Mental purification allows us to become more conscious of our daily thoughts and the attitudes that help to create them. It also makes us more aware of how our thoughts are often influenced by past experience, old attitudes, and conditioning from family, school, work, and the media.

Spiritual purification helps us to become more aware of our spiritual nature, our deep connection to Earth, and the reason why we are here in the world. It offers us a greater opportunity to view our lives as a spiritual journey and enables us to relate to ourselves and others as members of a community of souls.

JEWISH CLEANSING RITUALS

The laws of cleanliness have been observed by religious Jews since Biblical times, and ritual bathing has been an important practice in their approach to God. The noted medieval Jewish physician and teacher Maimonides stressed both the physical and spiritual importance of ritual baths, and religious or observant Jews traditionally practice three major forms of ritual bathing: washing the hands, washing the hands and feet, and total immersion.

Washing the hands is the most widespread form of ablution and is usually performed by immersing the hands in water up to the wrist or pouring water onto the hands from a pitcher. Known in Hebrew as *netilat yadahim* (taking water to the hands), it appears to have originated with the ancient practice of washing the hands before and after eating consecrated food. It is still widely observed by Orthodox Jews today before eating bread or before saying grace at a meal. Religious law also calls for washing the hands upon arising from sleep, after the elimination of bodily wastes, before offering daily prayers, or after having been in the presence of a dead body.

Washing the hands and feet was a requirement for the priests before participating in the Temple service, a practice based on the Lord's instructions to Moses in Exodus 30:17–20. Although rarely done today, hand and foot washing is occasionally practiced by Orthodox rabbis during important holidays such as Yom Kippur, Succot, and Rosh Hashana.

Total immersion is known in Hebrew as *tevilah*, and involves the act of taking a ritual bath in a *mikveh*. A mikveh (a collection of water) is essentially a pool or a bath of clear, running water from a natural spring or river, although sometimes rainwater is used instead.

Because the water is required to cover the entire body, a mikveh must have a minimum capacity of 120 gallons of water. It may not be prefabricated and brought to the bathing site but is either hewn into rock or put into the ground like a swimming pool. The mikveh must also be completely water-tight, as any leaks render it useless. In places where the water comes through underground pipes, the mikveh cannot use water that has been kept in a holding tank. Because placing a stopper in the mikveh turns it into a holding tank, it can only be emptied from above by hand or, nowadays, with the aid of an electric pump. The importance of a mikveh cannot be underestimated: In some Orthodox communities, constructing a mikveh is considered even more vital to the physical and spiritual life than a synagogue and is often the first religious structure to be built.

Bathing in a mikveh traces its origin to the ancient teachings of the Torah, which prescribe the need to remove uncleanness caused by leprosy, the discharge of semen apart from sexual intercourse, childbirth, contact with a corpse, or menstruation. The Torah prohibits sexual intercourse for seven "clean days" from the end of the woman's period, a state known as *niddah,* meaning "to be removed or separated." For most women, this means 12 days of sexual abstinence a month; in many religious homes, husband and wife aren't even allowed to sleep together, lest they forget themselves.

After carefully counting the days, the wife goes to the mikveh, usually after nightfall, often accompanied by her husband (the mikveh is usually staffed by a female attendant, often a volunteer). After cleaning herself thoroughly in a hot bath, the woman must remove all articles (including hairpins, bandages, rings, and even nail polish) that would constitute a barrier between the water and all parts of her body. Her hair is also washed and combed.

Upon entering the mikveh and immersing herself in an upright position, she recites the following prayer: "Blessed art Thou, Lord our God, King of the universe who has sanctified us with His commandments and commanded us concerning the immersion." After the prayer, the woman immerses herself totally in the water once again.

Jewish law also requires that one area of a mikveh should be used to cleanse pots, dishes, and other eating utensils. Before using certain utensils for eating, observant Jews believe they must first be sanctified, and the vessel will, in turn, sanctify the food served in it.

CHRISTIAN HOLY WATER

Early Christians followed the Jewish example of cleanliness, both symbolically and practically. The Prophets had already used the symbolism of bathing to express the idea of spiritual purification in the Old Testament books of Isaiah, Ezekial, and Zechariah, and John the Baptist walked his followers into the running waters of the sacred Jordan River as a symbolic act of washing away their sins, as expressed in Mark 1:4: "John the

Cleansing

The Jordan River at the site where Jesus is said to have been baptized

baptizer appeared in the wilderness, preaching a baptism of repentance for the forgiveness of sins." (Baptism will be discussed in the Initiation chapter.)

In Catholic churches, water blessed by a priest to symbolize spiritual cleansing is known as *holy water*. Through the medium of the water, the Church transfers a priest's blessing to the faithful. Roman Catholic churches traditionally place a font of holy water inside the entrance of the church so that parishioners can bless themselves with it on entering for mass—a gesture believed to wash away any venial sins.

Holy water was very important to Teresa of Avila, the sixteenth-century Spanish Carmelite nun, mystic, and visionary. Both humble and highly devout, Teresa experienced powerful spiritual visions. It has been said that the states of her prayers could be so intense that she often became alarmed; and convinced that she was not worthy of visitations from God, Teresa imagined that some of her visions were but delusions orchestrated by Satan: "At one time, too, I thought the evil spirits would have suffocated me one night. And when the sisters threw much holy water about I saw a great troop of them rush away as if tumbling over a precipice." A strong believer in the power of holy water, St. Teresa wrote about how it affected entities she associated with evil:

> I know by frequent experience that there is nothing which puts the devils to flight than holy water. They run away before the sign of the cross also, but they return immediately: great, then, must be the power of holy water. As for me, my soul is conscious of a special and most distinct consolation whenever I take it. Indeed, I feel almost always a certain refreshing, which I cannot describe, together with an inward joy, which comforts my whole soul. . . . I may compare what I feel with that which happens to a person in great heat, and very thirsty, drinking a cup of cold water—his whole being is refreshed.

One of the St. Teresa's most dramatic descriptions was of an encounter with the Devil himself and how both the holy water and her fervent prayers helped liberate tortured souls from purgatory:

I . . . was saying some very devotional prayers at the end of our Breviary, when Satan put himself on the book before me, to prevent my finishing my prayer. I made the sign of the cross and he went away. I then returned to my prayer, and he, too, came back; he did so, I believe, three times, and I was not able to finish the prayer without throwing holy water at him. I saw certain souls at that moment come forth out of purgatory—they must have been near their deliverance, and I thought that Satan might in this way have been trying to hinder their release. It is very rarely that I saw Satan assume a bodily form . . . .

While the visitations described by Teresa of Avila may seem rather extreme, holy water has brought tremendous comfort to practicing Catholics. Writing in *U.S. Catholic*, Tim Unsworth declared,

Before they put me into the ground, the priest will sprinkle the gaping grave with holy water. My grieving relatives will be relieved. Their sturdy faith will have convinced them that holy water can cool the fires of hell in a race for my soul. . . . My family will have to wait for Judgment Day to see if the water will have spared me. Meanwhile, the gesture with water will symbolize external cleansing and internal purification.

MUSLIM RITUAL WASHING

The Muslim practice of ritual cleansing, known as *faraid al-wudu*, is based on the teachings of the Holy Qur 'an IV.46, which reads, "O believers, when ye come to fulfill the prayer, wash your faces and your hands as far as the elbows; and rub your heads, and your feet unto the ankles." Ablution is considered a heartfelt act of obedience to Allah and is required before making one's five daily prayers: Like other forms of ritual bathing, faraid al-wudu adheres to a prescribed sequence involving first the washing of the hands, and then the head, followed by the feet. The practice of ritual bathing also observes a wide range of strict rules, which often vary according to the different schools of Islam. For example, the Jafari believe that when washing the hands, one must start from the elbows, and consider it obligatory to wash the right hand before the left; the Shafiis teach that one must not only wash the face, but also the area under the chin. The Hanbalis require that in addition to the hands, face, and feet, one must also rinse the mouth and draw water into the nose. As in Judaism and Christianity, purity of the ritual water is essential in all Muslim rites.

Total immersion bathing (*ghusl*) is practiced in cases of certain types of impurity and is recommended after sexual intercourse, nocturnal emission, menstruation, childbirth, conversion, and after washing a corpse. As in the Jewish mikveh, Islamic law requires that the water used in ghusl must touch all parts of the body, including every hair; yet in contrast to the mikveh, which is only used for ritual bathing, ghusls often take place in an ordinary plunge pool located in the local *hammam*.

The Hammam

The Muslim sweat bath—known as the *hammam*—remains one of the most important gathering places in the Islamic world today. In addition to serving as a major social center, many hammams are connected to mosques and are used for ritual purification, especially after an illness, a long journey, or a period of adversity. Muhammad was one of the first to promote the healing properties of the hammam and believed that the heat generated by the hammam enhanced fertility. Many traditional hammams are both spacious and beautiful, often featuring colored glass set in graceful domes to allow the entry of multicolored sunlight. Some hammams were constructed of rich materials such as marble and were decorated with mosaics and strong stone columns. Following the example of the Romans, who bathed in hot springs, some early hammams were heated by a pool of water from a natural hot spring that was constantly bubbling and flowing. Because Arabs traditionally disliked bathing in still water (which was perceived as bathing in one's own filth) the moving water in the hammam encouraged immersion bathing.

Although at first the hammam was the exclusive domain of Muslim men, women were later permitted to partake of the purifying bath; but entry was originally restricted to women who had already given birth. Over time it became such an important part of life for the Muslim woman that she had sufficient grounds for divorce if she was not permitted by her husband to visit the hammam.

Folklore in many Islamic cultures suggests that spirits called *jinn* dwell in the waters of springs, including those found in the hammam. Although some jinn were viewed as malicious or mischievous, others were believed to recite poetry and serve as protective guardians. Protection from malicious jinn was achieved by intoning a sacred invocation, avoiding bathing between the last two prayers of the day, or by painting religious symbols on the doors of the hammam.

HINDU PURIFICATION RITES

The Ganges is considered the holiest river in India, and written records referring to the merits of bathing in it go back to 634 C.E. Believed to be the body of the Goddess Ganga herself, the river represents the feminine energy of the universe that is connected to both life and death. According to Hindu belief, the Ganges purifies everything that it touches. Pilgrims come to the river believing that bathing in it will cleanse them of their sins and will allow them to take one step closer to freedom from the cycle of birth and death, to a blissful state known as *moksha.* Those who feel that death may be near sometimes make a pilgrimage to the Ganges, so that they can take a final bath, die, and have their remains cremated by her banks.

The Burning Ghats, Benares, 1892

Bones and ashes are scattered into the sacred river. There are Hindu priests who receive ashes by parcel post from other parts of India and ceremonially throw them into the sacred waters, thus purifying the deceased's entire being and allowing it to merge with the body and spirit of the goddess.

Pilgrims often practice ritual bathing at prominent *tirthas* (crossings) that mark the river's path, and the most important bathing sites are at the holy cities of Varanasi (Benares) and Hardwar. During the festival of Ganga Dussehra, which celebrates the descent of the Goddess Ganga to Earth, hundreds of thousands arrive at the river at sunrise for a ritual bath. For those who don't have access to the Ganges, a ritual bath in another river, lake, or pool is recommended; bathers traditionally enter the water chanting "Har Har Gange," thus invoking the power of the goddess. Bathing on this auspicious day is considered an important religious exercise that will wash away all sins.

Sacred Ganges water is traditionally offered to wedding guests in sealed copper containers; it is also utilized as a charm to repel evil spirits, is dripped into the mouths of the sick, and is considered a medium for taking oaths. Devout Hindus ritually pour a few drops of Ganges water into their daily baths, thus invoking Ganga's purifying powers at the start of each day. It is also given to a dying person along with *Tulsi* (basil) leaves in order to facilitate a peaceful transition.

HOLY WATER IN THAILAND

Holy water has various uses among the Thai. Although some 90 percent of the population consider themselves to be practicing Buddhists, many adhere to animistic beliefs that predate the arrival of Buddhism in Thailand. One widespread belief holds that spirit beings originally inhabited the site of a present-day home or business. As they build a new home, the human inhabitants seek to propitiate the spirits by giving them a home of their own, which takes the form of a miniature spirit house located next to the dwelling occupied by humans. Before a new spirit house is installed, a shaman sprinkles holy water on a piece of copper engraved with magical devices that has been placed at the base of the spirit house. Water is also commonly used for ritual exorcism, a delicate task performed by a specially trained Buddhist monk or Hindu Brahman priest, whose ancestors originally immigrated from India centuries ago. It is commonly believed that evil spirits loathe and fear water, and people who feel they are possessed by them undergo ritual bathing to help dislodge the malevolent entity. The angry spirit often causes the person to become so upset and violent during the bath that the bather may have to be physically restrained. After the exorcism is complete, the monk or priest creates a protective amulet for the person to wear.

SHINTO PURIFICATION

Ritual cleansing is also an important aspect of Shinto, the indigenous religion of Japan. Known as "the way of the kami" or "way of the deities," Shinto is a nature-based religion that contains an amalgam of attitudes, ideas, and practices that have influenced Japanese religious, social, and political life for thousands of years. In addition to ancestor worship, Shinto teaches the existence of deities that are connected to natural forms such as trees, mountains, and lakes.

Purification, known as *harai,* is one of the four elements of worship (the others being Prayer, Offering, and Symbolic Feast) and is performed to re-establish order and balance between nature, humans, and deities as well as to regularly remove the impurities from people that prevent their true spiritual nature from shining through. Harai is a vital part of all Shinto rituals and is practiced on special occasions throughout the year; it may be performed by a worshipper or by a Shinto priest.

First, a worshipper symbolically rinses the mouth and pours clear water on the fingertips, a ritual known as *temizu,* or hand water. A priest then recites a special prayer and waves a purification wand over the individual or group, which is accompanied by a light sprinkling of salt water. This is followed by the formal presentation of appropriate offerings (such as food, salt, water, or flowers) to a kami who often include one's ancestral spirits. Whole-body ritual bathing, known as *misogi,* is sometimes done before major religious ceremonies or important personal celebrations such as marriage and anniversaries.

Perhaps the most dramatic form of misogi is performed at the Tsubaki Grand Shrine, located at the foot of Mt. Takayama and Mt. Hikiyama in Mie Prefecture. Purification is achieved by standing under a pounding waterfall to purify the individual's *tama,* or soul. This powerful rite not only unites the person with the waterfall and its kami, but is also said to bring about communion with the creative life force of the universe, called *daishizen,* or Great Nature.

THE NATIVE AMERICAN SWEAT LODGE

Water has always been an important element of ritual cleansing for Native Americans. A unique cleansing ritual, called "Going to Water" was traditionally practiced by the Cherokee, Choctaw, and other southeastern peoples before a ritual ball game, a contest of both physical prowess and magical power. Performed in sacred streams, the body of each player would be scratched (some received up to 300 scratches) with a ceremonial comb made up of 7 sharp rattlesnake teeth. The bleeding player would then enter the stream and face east. Rinsing the blood from his body, the village shaman would pray that the player be given a clear mind, along with strength and agility.

The sacred sweat lodge ceremony is probably the most important cleansing ritual among Native Americans. Like the rites of other cultures, the purpose of the sweat lodge is to purify the body, mind, and soul, although it utilizes the water

Native American sweat lodge

element as steam as opposed to its liquid form. Every aspect of it is rich in spiritual meaning. The sweat lodge is often built or renovated on the day of the ceremony and is usually made of willow saplings—symbolic of birth and regeneration—which are placed in such a way as to mark off the four directions of the universe. The lodge itself is often formed in the shape of a dome or an oval, representing the womb of Mother Earth. A special pit, symbolizing the center of the universe, is dug for the placement of superheated rocks, which also represent the living Mother Earth. The entryway is set low, both to prevent heat from escaping and to teach humility, as participants often have to enter on their hands and knees.

Participants in the ceremony, which is usually segregated by sex, traditionally enter the lodge naked and take their seats in pitch darkness. This experience has been likened to a fetus in the womb, which in this case is the womb of Mother Earth. According to Medicine Grizzlybear Lake, a prominent medicine man and shaman, "We prefer to go into the sweat lodge stripped of all our clothes, symbols, badges of education, status and wealth, camouflages or all other coverings which feed the human ego. We go naked as a newborn into the womb of Mother Earth; humble, pure, innocent and prepared for nurturing." Medicine Grizzlybear teaches that spiritual intent is an important aspect of partaking in the sacred ceremony: "We try to strip ourselves of [defining] human qualities, desires and characteristics in order to become more spiritlike; we shed our human image and physical attributes in order to discover our soul and its spiritual nature. And, in most cases we come out reborn and re-created."

The sweat lodge ceremony is both emotionally and physically demanding. Cold water is poured on superheated rocks, which have carefully been brought inside. This makes the air (which has been described by shamans as "Divine Light Breath") both steamy and extremely hot; some participants find the heat practically unbearable, as breathing can become an arduous chore. During the ceremony, prayers are recited and sacred songs are chanted, sometimes accompanied by a flute. Offerings, such as tobacco, are placed on the hot stones, and a pipe may be passed around and smoked. Among groups such as the Creek, a "talking stick" is passed from person to person so that everyone has the opportunity to share thoughts, feelings, and stories with other participants.

Medicine people have reported that supernatural beings often visit the lodge during the sacred sweat ceremony. According to the Lakota medicine man Archie Fire Lame Deer, "They are usually invisible, but their presence is felt. Sometimes they make the sweat lodge shake violently. On rare occasions, medicine men who walk in balance with Earth can see and identify the spirits and understand their words."

Each individual takes away something unique from the ceremony; some experience a powerful emotional catharsis, while others may have visions and deep spiritual insights. The private ceremony described by Archie Lame Deer for a man who could neither speak nor hear is both magical and moving:

I took him inside the lodge. . . . It was not very hot, at least for me, but it seemed that for him the heat was unbearable. He made frantic signs, imploring me to open the flap and let him out. I signed back to him, "I want to hear you cry out loud. I want to hear you scream. I won't let you out until you fill this lodge with the sound of your voice." . . . I poured all the rest of the water on the rocks in one motion, making it real hot. Then, out of the deaf-mute came a mighty scream—like the first cry of a newborn—only much, much louder. It was the first cry that man had ever uttered in his life, and it was so piercing that it penetrated his deafness.

6

HEALING

Waters, yield your cure as an armor for my body, so I may see the sun for a long time.
—FROM A HINDU PRAYER

Healing is more than eliminating disease symptoms; it is a process of achieving wholeness, alignment, and integration that encompasses every level of our being. Healing encourages self-awareness and enables us to express our unique potential more fully in our work, study, and relationships with ourselves and others. The healing journey not only helps us connect to our own inner rhythms but also brings us closer to our spiritual nature and the world around us. According to psychiatrist George L. Hogben,

The spa in Wiesbaden, Germany

Healing may be defined as a miraculous unfolding of consciousness for one's being in the world. We learn who we are, what and who really matter to us, how to express ourselves fully and openly. Ultimately, the healing journey leads to an intimate union with God through the experience of the flow of God's spirit within. It is a slow, arduous passage, unique for each individual, filled with danger and risk, triumph and joy, and finally, peace, trust, awe, reverence, love, tenderness.

Water has been a powerful factor in healing since time immemorial. Sacred springs and wells have been used by the Celts, Greeks, Romans, Arabs, Japanese, Native Americans, and many other peoples. Some, such as Holywell in Wales or Zamzam near

Mecca, remain sacred pilgrimage sites, while ancient healing springs like Aix-les-Bains in France, Bath in England, and Wiesbaden in Germany have achieved fame as popular spas.

The Bible tells of several healing miracles related to water. In the Old Testament, we read of the miraculous healing of Na'aman, army commander to the King of Syria, who was suffering from leprosy. Na'aman was told by Elisha's messenger to wash himself in the waters of the Jordan River (2 Kings 5:10, 14): "So he went down and dipped himself seven times in the Jordan, according to the word of the man of God; and his flesh was restored like the flesh of a little child, and he was clean."

At the Pool of Bethesda in Jerusalem, it was believed that the angel of the Lord would occasionally descend from the heavens and touch the surface of the still water; after the angel's visit, the first person entering the pool would be cured of any illness. One day, we read in John 5:1–18, Jesus came upon a sick man lying near the pool and immediately healed him both physically and spiritually, taking on the role of God's angel.

WATER AND HEALTH

Water is highly therapeutic. There is the almost immediate sensation of comfort and relaxation as we settle into a bathtub filled with warm water or the dramatic awakening of the senses when we step into a cold shower. Water therapy is among the most ancient healing arts and includes literally hundreds of individual modalities.

Ritualized bathing dates back at least to Ancient Egypt and was an important rite among the early Hebrews, Greeks, and Romans. Hot-water baths relax and soothe and are popular for relieving body aches and pains. They help the body eliminate toxins, increase its metabolism, and raise its temperature in order to fight disease. However, long, hot baths can make us feel weak and exhausted and are generally not recommended. Cold water invigorates, energizes, and fortifies the body. It causes the blood vessels to constrict, thereby shunting blood to other parts of the body. At the same time, the brain tells the cardiovascular system to send fresh blood to the cold areas, resulting in fresh vitality and warmth. Some therapeutic bathing protocols use both hot and cold water to stimulate the nervous system.

Some healing baths involve only specific parts of the body, such as the feet or hands; others call for adding specific herbs and salts to the water, such as rosemary, nutmeg, bicarbonate of soda, or Epsom salts. Swirling waters—such as a whirlpool or Jacuzzi—often increase the therapeutic value of an ordinary bath and are prescribed to relieve pain, reduce tissue swelling, and increase circulation in both the limbs and body.

Showers are also utilized for healing and are applied at various temperatures and pressures. Cold showers, for example, are used therapeutically to stimulate the body, reduce temperature, and help overcome fatigue. Warm or hot showers help sedate the central nervous system, soothe irritated skin, and relieve pain. The *Vichy shower,* named after the French spa where it was first developed, uses several nozzles arranged in a horizontal pattern to create either a gentle or vigorous rain shower; it's especially popular in beauty treatments such as skin exfoliation and wet massage therapy. A simple but powerful showering technique is the *Scotch hose*, which shoots a powerful stream of water applied from 10 to 12 feet away. Skilled therapists use it to massage the bather in specific areas of the body to promote relaxation and healing.

Water packs and compresses both provide cooling and warming to afflicted parts of the body and often contain other healing elements such as herbs and salts. Cold packs are widely used as a tonic, sedative, and eliminative and help reduce fever, relieve joint pain, and alleviate skin problems, whereas hot packs are applied to increase body temperature and remove toxins. Hot, moist compresses also help relieve symptoms of gout and rheumatism.

Steam is water in its gaseous form. Because its high temperature promotes perspiration, steam opens the pores of the skin and helps eliminate toxins. Like the hot-water bath, steam baths help raise body temperature, which kills bacteria and viruses. They offer relief for muscle aches and sprains and also treat arthritis and joint problems. Steam—especially when used in a vaporizer—helps relieve breathing problems, colds, and sinus attacks.

HEALING SPRINGS

Healing springs are usually defined as springs of varying temperature that contain minerals, gases, and vapors that have specific therapeutic effects on the human body. These effects include increases in temperature, improved functioning of the glandular, digestive, and circulatory systems, strengthening of the immune system, relief of muscle pain, and improved skin tone.

Each country has its own system of classifying healing springs according to temperature, the levels of acidity or alkalinity, and the predominant minerals found in the water, such as carbon dioxide, magnesium, iron, or sulfur.

ANCIENT SOURCES

In times past, mineral and thermal springs inspired both fear and fascination. For many, water gushing up from an unknown source often awakened a very natural sense of wonder. Because they appeared to originate from deep within the earth, healing springs were considered the homes of powerful deities who controlled the forces of life and death. The Iroquois, who lived in what is now upstate New York, believed that the carbonated waters at High Rock Spring at Saratoga were stirred by their great god Manitou, thus endowing the spring with healing properties. In contrast, the Cahuilla people of California were convinced that the waters of what is now Palm Springs were populated by an enormous blue frog, a large snake, and other spirit beings who would cry like human infants if something bad was about to take place. The Cahuilla would pray and make offerings of food in order to ensure their safety whenever they would venture into the healing waters to bathe.

Healing

We humans have enjoyed bathing in mineral springs since time immemorial: Traces of *Homo erectus* dating back 600,000 years have been found in the vicinity of some hot springs in both Europe and the Middle East. Those rich in minerals such as sulfur, iron, and chloride often could be recognized by a distinctive color or odor that set them apart from ordinary springs. Many gained immediate notoriety for their apparent ability to heal wounds and relieve symptoms of arthritis and other diseases among those who bathed in them. Virtually all became known as sacred springs connected with a vast pantheon of spirit beings, including gods, goddesses, and other water deities.

The ancient Greeks enjoyed bathing in both private and public baths, and people such as Homer, Hippocrates, and Asclepiades stressed the importance of both drinking water and bathing in water for health. A famous spring in the ancient city of Thermae—today's Loutraki—was held to be favored by the gods and became the first health resort recorded in the annals of world history. The name *Thermae* comes from Artemis Thermia, the protectress of hot mineral springs. Both Apollo, the god of the sun and of spiritual peace, and Hera, the mother of the gods, were worshipped at temples there. The first written mention of the baths at Thermae is by Xenophon in his *Hellenica* in the fourth century B.C.E.

Healing springs were believed to be inhabited by spirits known as naiads, said to be daughters of Zeus and often depicted as beautiful young women possessing healing powers.

Usually, only one naiad resided in a sacred spring, although sometimes there could be up to two or three, considered sisters of equal rank. Sick people would primarily drink the sacred water, although some would occasionally bathe in the spring as well. Visitors were respectful of the resident naiads, who were viewed as guardians of the sacred water and responsible for its healing properties; any offenses could induce illness, especially paralysis and insanity. Allegedly the Roman emperor Nero once experienced temporary paralysis and fever after bathing in the sacred Marium Spring in Rome, and his illness was attributed to his having offended the resident naiads.

As mentioned in the previous chapter, Romans were tremendously fond of bathing for both health and pleasure, and Roman baths, often expensive and luxurious establishments, served as places of entertainment, gymnastics, relaxation, and debate. As they conquered new lands, the Romans discovered numerous thermal and mineral springs and transformed them into a network of baths, or aquae. Many of them became centers for colonization and development. Roman baths extended from Bath *(Aquae Sulis)* and Epsom in England and Wales to France, Germany, Switzerland, and Italy as well as today's Romania, Hungary, Slovenia, Bulgaria, and Turkey.

Many of these springs were connected to Celtic and then Roman gods and goddesses that represented both water *and* sun: The presiding divinity of the bountiful springs at Bath in England (which wells up at an astounding quarter million gallons a day) was Sulis-Minerva—a combination of Sulis (known to the Celts as both healer and avenger as well as the personification of healing water), and Minerva Medica, the healing aspect of the Roman goddess of arts and crafts.

Supplanting the deity of a conquered people with that of the victor has been common practice, in Europe and elsewhere, since prehistoric times. In France, for example, the Celtic deities Nerius, Ibosus, and Epona were associated with the healing springs at Neris but were later replaced by the Roman god Mercury. Apollo supplanted the Celtic gods Borvo and Damona as the guardian of the springs at Bourbonne. Sacred springs and wells were often important pilgrimage sites. During the first century B.C.E., visitors to the spring at Chamalières in central France (known today as Royat-Chamalières, a spa specializing in the treatment of heart and circulatory disease) would offer wooden votive models of themselves or the affected part of their bodies to the resident deity known either as Ovh or Ovhanna.

There is strong evidence that many pre-Christian healing wells passed from one faith to another as the people themselves embraced Christianity. If the waters were viewed as a gift of the divine, even if the understanding of who or what constitutes the divine changed, the gift remained. Thus bodies of water that were sacred to the pre-Christian peoples of Europe often became sites for Christian churches, monasteries, and convents. One such site was at Luxeuil in France, where Saint Columban founded a monastery. Not surprising, followers of the old and the new faith tended to eye each other with suspicion. Jonas, an early Christian observer, left us a very subjective description of pagan Luxeuil: "There were hot springs there, held in devout reverence; stone images crowded its forest glades, honoured in ancient days by the pitiful cult and impious ceremonial of the heathen people of this countryside, who offered before them their accursed rites." Under Columban, Luxeuil continued as a Christian healing site, and today, Luxeuil-les-Bains is a popular health resort specializing in the treatment of phlebitis and gynecological conditions.

Bathing in sacred springs has also been popular in Japan for thousands of years. Tradition says that people were acquainted with them since 700 B.C.E., with springs at Atami, Shuzenji, Suwa, and Dogo among the most ancient. Like those in Europe, many of the early Japanese medicinal springs were believed to be the abode of spiritual beings (known in Japan as kami), and their discovery, often by Buddhist priests and other holy people on pilgrimage, was perceived as a sign of spiritual vision and divine guidance. Sometimes animals that were regarded as messengers of the gods would be of assistance. The discovery of the healing waters at Takeo on Kyushu Island was attributed to the Empress Jingu, who came upon a white heron taking a bath in the warm waters. The ancient Kage springs on Honshu Island were known as the Springs of Monju, because a wounded deer that was found near the springs was believed to be an incarnation of Monju Bosatsu (also known as Manjusri Bodhisattva), the Buddhist God of Wisdom. Other discoveries were believed to be the result of divine intervention: A sick person would pray for healing, be given an oracle as a dream, and would take a successful journey into the mountains to the springs that had been revealed there. Many such prayers were offered to Yakushi Nyorai and Dainichi Nyorai, two divine healers of Buddhism who later became important Shinto gods of medicine.

The healing properties of hot springs in Japan were documented by both poets and early regional chronicles. Describing the curative powers of the Tamatsukuri Hot Spring, in Shimane Prefecture (known for its sodium bicarbonate and calcium-sulfate waters), the chronicle *Isumo Fudoki* reported that by "bathing once, the visitor was made fair of face and figure;

Small shrine near Umijigoku Springs, Beppu, Japan

bathing twice, all diseases were healed; its effectiveness has been obvious since the days of old." The early Japanese developed a growing appreciation for bathing in mineral springs, which were given names such as Meniyo (eye bath), Hiji-ori (elbow broken), or Tano-yu (ringworm bath) to identify their specific curative properties. Shinto shrines can still be found next to many hot springs in Japan, testifying to the presence of the kami, believed to inhabit a spring and guide its evolution. Even today, visitors to hot springs often give thanks to the kami for the water's healing powers.

Native Americans have always considered mineral springs to be sacred healing grounds. Anthropological evidence uncovered at Lake Amatitlán near Guatemala City revealed that the Maya may have used thermal springs as early as 500 B.C.E. Among the Aztecs, lakes, rivers, and springs were considered the abodes of gods and goddesses. Because water was so highly regarded as essential to life in an area subject to frequent droughts, mothers of newborn babies often prayed to these divinities for their children's protection and healing. The hot springs in central Mexico were important places of pilgrimage for Aztec priests and nobility; the sulfur-rich waters at Agua Hedionda (stinking water) near Cuautla in Morelos State were frequented by Montezuma and other Aztec leaders for both physical and spiritual renewal. Many of these ancient springs can still be enjoyed today, although the primitive watering holes have been replaced by Olympic-size swimming pools, whirlpool baths, and water slides.

Farther north, the area now known as Hot Springs in Arkansas was originally called Valley of the Vapors, and was a sacred site of peace and healing for the Tunicas people. The Spanish explorer Hernando DeSoto is believed to have been the first European to visit these springs, in 1541. He described it as a place where members of warring groups could be found bathing, trading, and sharing meals in harmony. Sacred springs served as "peace sites" throughout much of North America and were often used for arranging marriages, resolving inter-tribal differences, and negotiating peace treaties.

Many native peoples of North America believed that hot springs were gifts of the Great Spirit who warmed them with his breath. Because tribal elders taught that the springs were the home of magical beings who could both heal and destroy, entering a hot spring was shrouded in ceremonial practice and decorum and respect were observed by all visitors. The Iroquois, Shawnee, and Tuscarora peoples often bathed together in Medicine Springs in what is now Bedford, Pennsylvania. Today's Harbin Hot Springs in Lake County, California, were used by the Lake and Coast Miwok peoples as a seasonal camp and sacred ground, with the hot springs being a place of healing, of negotiating treaties, and as a portal of entry to the spiritual realms. According to Ellen Klages,

> ...to a shaman, the waters of a hot springs were an entrance way to the underworld. In a trance state, induced by meditating on such a point of entrance—a natural tunnel, rock crevasse or spring—a shaman could travel from

the material world to the spirit realm. There he could talk to spirits and do healing work which, when returning to a non-trance state, be brought back to the people of his tribe. Since these natural openings to the spirit world are rare, the springs were considered to be a very special and sacred point in the already sacred material world.

BALNEOLOGY

Unlike today, when literally thousands of medications are available to cure nearly every ailment known to humanity, eighteenth- and nineteenth-century physicians had access to a very limited repertory of drugs. Being aware of the healing powers that were popularly associated with certain springs, they took careful note of the waters' therapeutic effects and developed a systematic approach to bathing. These early observations were the foundation for the modern practice of *balneology*, a natural approach to health and healing that uses hot spring water, gases, mud, and climatic factors (such as heat) as therapeutic elements.

Bathing

Immersing oneself in mineral water is the most popular form of balneology. Therapeutic bathing may involve soaking in water at neck-level, as we would do in an ordinary swimming

Bathing at Hot Springs, Florida, 1968

pool, for approximately 15 to 20 minutes 2 or 3 times a day. Many people enjoy standing or sitting under a fountain of warm mineral water, as do these bathers at a mineral spring in Florida.

In addition to bathing, healing modalities such as hydrotherapy, mud therapy, physical therapy, massage, steam baths, physical exercises, inhalation of water vapor, and drinking mineral water are often used as part of a holistic program to preserve health and treat disease.

Inhaling

Inhaling mineral water as vapor can be effective in helping treat asthma, sinus problems, allergies, and other respiratory problems. In some European spa clinics, the mineral water is administered as mist through an oxygen mask or with the type of inhaler asthma patients use when taking medication. In spas like Bad Wildbad in Germany's Black Forest, the water is released from a fountain equipped with a special mist-producing nozzle: You stand over the fountain, push a button, and inhale a fine spray. It is also currently standard medical practice to recommend humidifiers for individuals with asthma and chronic sinusitis.

Drinking

The "drinking cure" is especially popular in European spas such as Vittel, Vichy, Loutraki, and Karlovy Vary (Carlsbad), where mineral water is also bottled for commercial use. After being examined by a spa physician, the patient stops by the source of the spring (which is often a beautiful pavilion) several times a day where he or she drinks a prescribed amount of mineral water.

Minerals from spring water are absorbed into the bloodstream via the digestive tract. By providing vital nutrients such as calcium, magnesium, iron, and zinc, they have a wide range of therapeutic effects on the cardiovascular, gastrointestinal, and nervous systems.

The drinking cure was known to American Indians as well. An Iroquois myth describes how Nekumonta saved his wife Shanewis and their people from a deadly plague by bringing them healing water. Venturing into the forest to find medicinal herbs, the young man walked for three days without eating. After stumbling over a fallen branch, he fell asleep. Because Nekumonta was a good man who respected the animals, trees, and even the flowers of the forest, a group of animals and tree spirits watched over him during his slumber and appealed to the Great Manitou to help the Iroquois save his wife from the plague. In his dream, he envisioned a beautiful waterfall that spoke the following: "Seek us, O Nekumonta, and when you find us, Shanewis shall live. We are the healing waters of the Great Manitou."

After searching in vain for a waterfall, Nekumonta realized that he had to dig instead for the promised waters. He dug for hours until he was utterly exhausted and eventually found a hidden spring. He drank from it, and his strength soon returned.

Nekumonta then fashioned a small vessel out of clay so he could bring some of the healing water to his wife. He rushed back home, told the others about the miracle spring and gave them directions, and found his beloved Shanewis close to death. Nekumonta forced some of the water through her lips, and she fell into a deep sleep. The next morning, Shanewis awoke completely healed. The whole group was freed of the plague that day and gave Nekumonta the title Chief of the Healing Waters.

One of the most important sacred sites in the Christian world is the holy grotto of Lourdes in southwestern France. In February 1858, a peasant girl named Bernadette Soubirous had

Taking water from the grotto at Lourdes

the first of nineteen apparitions of the Virgin Mary, who emerged from a small grotto; by the ninth apparition, Mary revealed a small spring to Bernadette that soon became known for its powerful healing qualities. The first documented cure occurred after the thirteenth apparition of the Virgin Mary and involved a blind stonecutter whose sight was restored after washing his eyes with the miraculous water.

Today, this small spring attracts thousands of pilgrims daily—many of whom venture to Lourdes in search of a miracle cure. Visitors can collect Lourdes water from spigots located at the grotto. Many take it home as a souvenir, for drinking, or for ceremonial use. Some pilgrims stay for several days to receive medical treatment in a small hospital, where baths of Lourdes water are given in addition to traditional medical care.

A medical bureau was organized in 1882 to provide scientific verification of the cures, especially for diseases that had previously been determined incurable by physicians. By the year 2000 more than 5,000 "miraculous" cures had been documented for which there was no simple scientific or natural explanation.

HOLY WELLS, HEALING WELLS

Like springs, wells have always been revered as places of spiritual nourishment and healing, including Mary's Well in Nazareth, believed to be where the Virgin Mary drew water to sustain the child Jesus. Because many early civilizations originated in regions where water was often scarce and difficult to find, it was perceived as a gift from the heavens.

Carrying water from Mary's Well, Nazareth

The Romans revered wells, which existed throughout the Empire, and shrines were often built next to them. One, dedicated to the goddess Coventina, was located near a fort along Hadrian's Wall in Britain. Excavations in the nineteenth century showed that this well was an important ceremonial site that was visited by many thousands of people, who often left offerings of coins to the goddess. Archeological evidence from a sacred well in Sorgenti di Vicarello in Italy revealed that humans had worshipped there since prehistoric times: Archaeologists first came across brass and silver coins dating from the fourth century that were given as offerings. Deeper down, they found gold and silver coins dating from the reign of Emperor Augustus (27 B.C.E.–14 C.E.); going still deeper, there were layers of coins dating to the early Roman city-state (450 B.C.E.), while the deepest strata of material revealed arrowheads and knives made from polished stone.

Thousands of sacred wells used to be known in Europe, many of them in Celtic lands; Ireland alone once had an estimated 3,000 of them. Sacred Celtic trees, such as the yew, were often planted near holy wells, symbolizing the promise of healing, regeneration, and eternal life.

One of the most famous of the old Celtic sites is Saint Winifrid's well in the town of Holywell on the northern coast of Wales. Cut into the hillside, just below the medieval parish church, the well is completely encased in a late fifteenth-century shrine. One of the few sacred wells that has survived the onset of Reformation and Rationalism, its history is rich in myth and legend.

Probably a sacred pagan site dating back thousands of years, a twelfth-century Christian legend tells us that the well came into being when Winifrid, a young princess, was accosted by a local chief named Caradoc. Determined to preserve her virtue, Winifrid resisted his advances, and Caradoc drew his sword in anger and struck off her head. Where Winifrid's head fell a spring immediately arose—the spring that feeds the well.

Hearing her screams, a priest and future saint named Beuno, who was the spiritual counselor to her father's court, came running, picked up her head and restored her to life. Over the years, both Beuno and Winifrid returned periodically to the well to bless it, promising that pilgrims coming there would receive whatever they prayed for.

Another famous well in Wales is St. Beuno's Well, reputed to have the power to heal children's diseases, especially rashes and other skin problems. Chapel Wells in Kirkmaiden Parish, Scotland, is a series of fresh-water wells consisting of three natural cavities that often fill with sea water during high tide. Dr. Robert Trotter visited this well in 1870 and observed the following healing ritual:

> The child [who was described as "sickly"] was stripped naked, taken by one of the legs, and plunged headforemost into the big well till completely submerged: it was then pulled out, and the leg used to hold the child submerged in the middle well. Finally, the eyes were washed in the

smallest well. The entire procedure was altogether like the Achilles and Styx business, only much more thorough. An offering was then left in the old chapel, on a projecting stone inside the cave behind the west door, and the cure was complete.

Because water is so precious in the desert, every well takes on a great significance. The most famous holy well in the Arabian desert is Zamzam, located near the holy city of Mecca. Legend has it that Zamzam came forth due to the grace of God, who sent the angel Jibreel (Gabriel) in a time of dispair:

> Hazrat Hajira [known to the Jews as Hagar, the second wife of Abraham] and Hazrat Ismail [Ishmael, the son of Abraham] had to settle down in an area barren of water and vegetation. When the last of their food had finished, a mother's love for her distressed son could not be contained and so she undertook dashing from Safa to Marwa in search of sustenance. On her seventh trip, whilst she was on Marwa, she heard the noise of an angel and saw that a spring had emerged by his heels. This blessed water became food for Hazrat Hajira, which in turn became a source of milk for Hazrat Ismail.

The Prophet Muhammad is said to have drunk from the well and to have carried its water in leather canteens and clay bottles to pour on the heads of the sick; he also had them drink the water, often with miraculous healing results.

Now covered with a dome, the sacred well of Zamzam remains extremely popular with Muslim pilgrims *(hajjis)*, who drink its water after taking their journey to Mecca. The well is also visited by those seeking a cure for illness or relief from poverty or other misfortune. One old saying goes: "Zamzam is a cure and a solution for all matters."

The water of Zamzam is believed to nourish a person like food, and Muhammad is quoted as saying: "The best water on the face of the Earth is the water of Zamzam. It satisfies in place of food and it is a cure from illness."

Water from this sacred well has recently been tested in European laboratories and compared to municipal water from the city of Mecca. Zamzam water was found to contain a higher concentration of calcium and magnesium salts, which may contribute to its reputed medicinal effects on the stomach, liver, and kidneys. The Saudi chemical engineer Moin Uddin Ahmed, who was called upon by King Faisal to scientifically analyze Zamzam's water in 1971, postulated that the presence of mineral salts may be why the water refreshes tired hajjis. He also pointed out that because the water contains fluorides, it may provide effective germicidal action that benefits the entire human organism. In addition to being consumed by pilgrims on site, Zamzam water is bottled and shipped to devout Muslims throughout the world.

7

INITIATION

*Air is the Vital Force, Water the Progenitor, the
vast Earth the Mother of All; Day and Night
are nurses, fondling all creation in their lap.*
— GURU NANAK,
THE FOUNDER OF SIKHISM

Initiation is an ancient rite of passage that marks a
"new beginning": an entrance into a different way of
being or a transition to expanded consciousness. It may
be an initiation into adulthood or entry into a deeper
level of spiritual understanding. Traditionally, initiation
involves ceremony. Ceremony enables the participants
to better see, hear, and understand the meaning of the
initiation itself, and achieve a deeper knowledge of the
inner essence that dwells beyond the outer form.

Throughout the world, human societies have viewed water as essential to the process of initiation; ceremonies and symbols of ritual washing have appeared in the religions of humankind at many different times and in many different places. Sacred rivers, springs, waterfalls, and lakes have been sites of spiritual pilgrimage and have often played a role in initiation rituals connected with birth, puberty, marriage, and fertility in many of the world's religious traditions. Sacred water has also been at the center of blessing and purifying the dead as their souls initiate their journey into the afterlife. A great Western tradition is the Christian rite of baptism.

BAPTISM

From the scrolls discovered at Qumran we know that at the time of Jesus, Judaism had developed various baptismal rites, even though none of them had replaced circumcision as the rite of initiation into the community. Christian contact with these rites came through the work of John the Baptist. According to A. N. Wilson, "...it has been plausibly suggested that John might once have been a member of the Qumran sect, or the Essenes, and then separated himself from his fellow sectarians in order to go into the desert—first as a solitary and then as a great, popular religious leader." Mark tells us that "John the Baptist appeared in the desert proclaiming a baptism of repentance for the forgiveness of sins. People of the whole Judean countryside and all the inhabitants of Jerusalem were

The baptism of Jesus

going out to him and were being baptized by him in the Jordan River as they acknowledged their sins. John was clothed in camel's hair, with a leather belt around his waist. He fed on locusts and wild honey." (1:4–6)

The Gospels describe the baptism of Jesus by John in the sacred Jordan River, as a momentous initiation rite in which Jesus was commissioned as a Servant of Yahweh: "It happened in those days that Jesus came from Nazareth of Galilee and was baptized in the Jordan by John. On coming up out of the water he saw the heavens being torn open and the Spirit, like a dove, descending upon him." (Mark 1:9–11)

For early Christians, baptism did not only signify a spiritual birth, but also symbolized the mystery of eternal life in which the individual "died" to his or her present existence in order to be reborn into a new life of at-one-ment with Christ and God.

Even crossing the Jordan became deeply symbolic to early Church leaders: According to the Alexandrian school of Christianity, wading through the Jordan into Israel was a highly important act of Christian initiation as the candidate entered into the land of promise.

To this day, adult baptism is a powerful rite of passage in which the recipient makes a profession of faith, declaring that Jesus is the Son of God, Lord, and Messiah. Baptism not only heralds rebirth, but also involves forgiveness of sin. It unites the person with the Mystical Body of Christ, and bestows the blessings of the Holy Spirit. According to John, the importance of baptism was addressed by Jesus himself: "Unless a man be reborn again of water and the Spirit, he cannot enter into the kingdom of God." (3:5) And in Matthew we read of Jesus' postresurrection command to baptize in the name of the Father, the Son, and the Holy Spirit (28:19–20).

In the early Church, baptism was done by total immersion; in fact, the individual was immersed in water three times to signify the Holy Trinity: the Father, the Son, and the Holy Spirit. Originally, because the person was likened to a baby who was being reborn, wearing clothing was generally discouraged. However, while clothing is always worn out of modesty today, some celebrants abstain from wearing jewelry out of respect for the edict of St. Hippolitus delivered more than 1,800 years ago: "Let them . . . put aside any gold and silver ornaments they may be wearing. Let no one take any foreign objects into the water with him."

Although a river was traditionally the preferred location for a baptism, other water sources, such as lakes and ponds, have been used as well.

Early baptismal fonts often took the form of a cross or a circle, although some, dating from Roman times, consisted of a circular basin carved out of a square block of stone; others were carved from blocks in the form of a star, trefoil, or quatrefoil. In Europe during the Middle Ages, fonts were often large circular stone bowls (some mounted on pedestals) richly carved with religious figures, regional legends, or biblical

Baptismal font, Aquileia, Italy

scenes from the Old and New Testaments or the Apocrypha. Many are still in use today.

The size of a baptismal font or pool varies considerably. While the majority hold just one person, larger ones are also used throughout the Christian world (the baptismal font at the Mormon Tabernacle in Salt Lake City is said to be large enough to accommodate hundreds of people).

Modernization has led many denominations to abandon total immersion in favor of *infusion,* or the pouring of water over the forehead of the person to be baptized. For the baptism of infants, the parents, godparents, and family members gather around the font with the baby and are asked by the priest or minister to affirm their belief in Christ and renounce evil. Holding the child, the minister blesses the water and says the words (as the water is being poured or sprinkled), "I baptize you in the name of the Father and of the Son and of the Holy Spirit."

In many mainstream Catholic and Protestant churches today, baptism is performed during a regular Sunday service when the infant is between three and four months of age. An Anglican or Episcopal baptism may conclude with readings from *The Book of Common Prayer,* while a Catholic baptism ends with the Lord's Prayer. Though a solemn event, a baptism traditionally brings great joy to family and friends and is cause for celebration: After the service everybody adjourns to the parish hall or a local restaurant for a party or luncheon.

The Roman rite often prescribes adding salt to holy water in the baptism of both infants and adults because the early

Romans believed that salt both cleanses the spirit and exorcises malevolent energies. This practice may be connected to that of Eliseus throwing salt into the unhealthy springs of Jericho during Biblical times in order to cleanse them of evil, or more probably, to the cleansing use of salt in religious ritual by pre-Christian Romans.

Among the Scots, water was often drawn from sacred wells for the baptism of infants. In Aberdeen, water was traditionally collected from St. Machar's Well and poured into the baptismal font at the nearby cathedral. In Renfrewshire, mothers took their sick or crippled children to St. Fillan's Well for baptism and in the hope of a miraculous cure.

During the Easter Vigil, specifically after the reading of scripture, the blessing of the baptismal water traditionally takes place. The entire ceremony, whose symbolic actions originated during the Middle Ages, is rich in imagery. According to the *New Catholic Encyclopedia,*

> . . . its general theme is that the water, made productive by the Spirit, gives birth to the divine life in men. The font is compared to a womb; it is the womb of Holy Church producing a heavenly offspring conceived in holiness and reborn as a new creation. During the consecratory Preface the priest plunges the candle into the water to show that the waters of Baptism derive their power to sanctify from the Passion and Resurrection of Christ. He pours in the chrism to symbolize the sanctification of the water by the Holy Spirit who is said to dwell in the chrism.

INITIATION INTO ADULTHOOD IN AFRICA

East and Central African peoples have traditionally utilized water in initiation ceremonies for boys and girls as they enter adulthood. Among the Yao and Makua peoples of Masasi in Tanzania, for example, *Lupanda* is the primary initiation ceremony for boys; the name itself is taken from a local tree with many branches. In some parts of the ceremony, both the young initiates and their parents participate: In preparation for the initiation, parents are called out of their homes by the sponsors of each boy undergoing initiation and are immediately splashed with water from a home-made pipe. Within a short time, the entire village gets involved in the ritual, with people noisily splashing each other at random.

After a night away from home, the boys undergo ritual bathing with the help of an older woman, who also assists in a ritual symbolic of the sexual act. According to anthropologists T. O. Ranger and Isaria Kimambo, "Near dawn the boys had to take a special bath at which a specially chosen lady would pour water on the back of each boy . . . after the bath, the boy and the lady, who then becomes his 'sister' had to perform another ceremony in which both hold a pestle and pound together in a mortar."

The traditional initiation ceremony for girls is called *Chiputu*, which includes instruction on how to manipulate the *labia minora* in order to enjoy sex with their future husbands. One local observer described the water-related aspects of the ritual: "The girls' bodies were washed with wet husks to make their skins lighter and beautiful and it was lovely to see them coming out looking so beautiful. The girls were given a proper bath in the morning of the day of coming out; they were given new clothes and their bodies were veiled." The observer added that at the conclusion of the ceremony, the girls would perform a type of belly dance to attract the attention of the newly initiated young men, who often chose the best dancers as their future wives.

The Dagara in Western Africa have a profound respect for water, which they believe is the abode of powerful deities. They also consider water to be essential to both the religious experience and the mystical journey. During his youth, Malidoma Patrice Somé experienced a powerful initiation ritual that involved plunging into a sacred spring that was perceived as an opening to the underworld. To this day he remembers the advice given to the young initiates by a Dagara elder, the facilitator for the initiation rite: "This water has been here since time immemorial. It protects the doorway to the ancestors. Only the sick are brought here for healing. This water is the roof of the world you are going to visit for awhile. You will jump into the pool one after the other. There is no bottom as there is in the village river, instead there is a world. When you jump in, do not waste your time in the watery area or you will drown. You will have to let yourself sink down as fast as you can until you stop. If you still have fear, let it go or you will drown.

A powerful Dagara cleansing ritual is the so-called Decontamination Rite. At the same time, it functions as a periodic initiation that can transform the consciousness of all participants. It usually takes place by a flowing stream that is decorated with flowers and other plants. Each participant obtains the branch of a tree, a smaller plant, or a piece of stone that is reputed to filter impurities in the water. The leader prays to the Spirit of Nature to enter the bodies and run through the veins and arteries of the celebrants in order to cleanse them of all impurities; the Spirit of Nature is also asked to join hands with the Spirit of Water. After invocation and chanting, the leader enters the water, followed by the other celebrants. He and his assistants splash water on them with the branches they originally brought to the ceremony. The leader and his aides then perform this splashing ritual on each other, and then everyone comes together for a closing prayer, thanking the spirits for their beneficence and acknowledging that the benefits of the cleansing will eventually reveal themselves in how each participant lives his life in the future.

THE TIBETAN WATER INITIATION

Water plays an important role in the sacred Kalachakra "Wheel of Time" ceremony of Tibetan Buddhism, a powerful rite of initiation, purification, and benediction believed to "clear away the defilement of evil deeds" in a person's life. Until recently, Kalachakra was reserved for only a few chosen disciples; however, the growing violence in the world inspired Buddhist teachers to make it available to larger groups of people in the hope of enabling them to awaken their "Buddha nature" and achieve enlightened peace for the benefit of all sentient beings.

The Kalachakra *mandala*, a large circular design representing the cosmos and chambers in which various Buddhist deities reside (symbolizing specific aspects of the Enlightened Mind), is central to this ritual. Practitioners use the mandala to visualize in meditation the steps along the Path to Enlightenment. Also known as the Palace of Deities, more than 700 gods and goddesses, or manifestations of the supreme deity Kalachakra, are portrayed within a circle of approximately 6 feet in diameter in the form of miniature human, animal, and plant forms, along with abstract pictographs

Kalachakra mandala

and Sanskrit syllables. The sand is made from white stones that are finely ground and mixed with opaque water colors.

Although it is no longer necessary for each person to undergo an initiation rite in order to view the sacred mandala, the viewing traditionally forms the culmination of a twelve-day ritual, which contains seven initiation rites (including those known as the Crown, Silk Ribbon, and Vajra), each enabling the disciple to attain a specific level of spiritual growth and attainment.

Taken together, these seven ceremonies are often referred to as Water Initiation because each involves the ritualized use of sanctified water, which is placed in a sacred vase in the shape of a conch shell. The water symbolizes the essence of various deities and the spiritual qualities they represent, including generosity, self-discipline, patience, effort, meditative stabilization, and wisdom. In addition to representing the deities, the water is considered to possess strong purifying qualities, and its use in Kalachakra is compared to the mother's first washing of her newborn child.

At a point during each ceremony, which includes the reciting of sacred verses or mantras, the lama blesses the disciple by gently touching a water-filled conch to the crown of his or her head, as well as the shoulders, upper arms, thighs, and hips. This is followed by the ritual sprinkling of the water on the five places that have been blessed, which is not only intended to suffuse the candidate with the spiritual essence of the deities but also to help eliminate all obstructions to enlightenment.

The process is finalized by the candidate ceremonially drinking the sacred water, which is said to generate intense feelings of joy and union with the heavenly realms.

The Water Initiation is not only intended to create feelings of bliss and enlightenment but also to provide the disciple with the wisdom and compassion to serve as a powerful agent for good in his or her daily life, and to help establish lasting peace in the world.

WATER AND THE TRANSITION INTO DEATH

Next to birth, the transition from life to death is perhaps the most important journey a human being can experience. In many of the world's cultures, water plays an essential role in this final initiatory process. We mentioned earlier how ritual cleansing in the Ganges (especially at the sacred cities of Hardwar and Benares) purifies the faithful of their sins and takes them a step nearer to spiritual liberation, known in Sanskrit as *moksha*. Many devout Hindus go to tremendous effort to experience this sacred bath as close to the time of their death as possible, so that they can more easily cross over the portal from life to death and finally, immortality. Many Hindus undertake a pilgrimage to the river at Benares to cremate their loved ones and deposit their ashes into the sacred river to merge with both the physical and spiritual essence of the river goddess Ganga.

The Old English epic *Beowulf* describes the water burials of the hero Scyld of the Sheaf and that of the beloved god Baldur, known as Giver of all Good. Scyld originally came to Denmark from across the sea as a baby laying in a boat, with his head resting on a sheaf of corn. Scyld later introduced agriculture to the Danes, who revered him as their king. When the beloved hero died, his body was sent back to the sea in a boat laden with treasure for his final journey to heaven.

The body of Baldur, after being murdered by the crafty Loki, the personification of evil in Nordic mythology, was placed in a boat that was launched and then set on fire, thus combining water burial with ritual cremation.

Water burials were also important among the ancient Mesopotamians, Africans, Polynesians, and Goths. According to anthropologist Donald A. Mackenzie:

> In the early part of the fifth century C.E. the Goths in Calabria diverted the course of the River Vasento, and having made a grave in the midst of its bed, where the course was most rapid, they interred their king with a prodigious amount of wealth and riches. They then caused the river to resume its regular course, and destroyed all persons who had been concerned in preparing this royal grave.

Some Native American peoples buried their dead by either tying stones to the deceased's body and sinking it in a lake, river, or spring or by setting the body afloat in a canoe and hoping that the person's soul would reach the land of the ancestors. Some groups believed that the canoe symbolized the womb of the water goddess from which the soul would be reborn in a future life. One Chinook canoe burial was described by George Catlin, who was best known for his sympathetic journals and beautiful paintings of Native Americans during the nineteenth century. He reported that in the burial of young children, their cradle often served as a canoe, which was floated in a sacred lake or pool. For deceased adults, the canoes were packed with food, hunting implements, blankets, and sacred tobacco, along with paddles to propel the canoes, and ladles to bale them out during the long journey to the next world.

8

WISDOM

Water, verily, is greater than food . . . .
Meditate on Water.

—CHHANDOGYA UPANISHAD

Water and wisdom have been associated since antiquity. The early Jews compared the sacred teachings of the Torah to water, and in Jeremiah 2:13, the Lord is called "the fountain of living waters." In Isaiah 55:1, the Prophet summons the people to listen to the word of God in the appeal "Ho, every one who thirsts. Come to the waters."

Spiritual teachers around the world have reflected on the instructive qualities of water. For many of them, it represented sensitivity, deep emotions, changeability, adaptability, and responsiveness. The symbolism of water was not lost on the early Chinese, who were well acquainted with its power, incorporating water-related elements into the philosophy and practice of Feng Shui. One eleventh-century C.E. Chinese scholar wrote:

> Of all the elements, the Sage should take water as his Preceptor. Water is yielding but all-conquering. Water extinguishes Fire or, finding itself likely to be defeated, escapes as steam and reforms. Water washes away soft Earth or, when confronted by rocks, seeks a way around. . . . It saturates the atmosphere so that Wind dies. Water gives way to obstacles with deceptive humility, for no power can prevent it following its destined course to the sea. Water conquers by yielding; it never attacks but always wins the last battle.

In ancient Greece, water gods such as Oceanus and Pontus, who lived in glimmering caves under the ocean, often denoted qualities of intelligence, because the Greeks associated knowledge with the immensity and depths of the ocean and seas. Nereus, the son of Pontus, was depicted in Greek myth as a genial old man of the sea who was distinguished for his gifts of prophesy and wisdom. Married to one of the daughters of Oceanus, he fathered no less than 50 daughters, known as the nereids; one of them married Poseidon, the brother of Zeus, thus uniting both the Older and Younger dynasties of the rulers of the sea.

In Celtic spirituality, water was viewed as a source of sustenance and healing, as well as a font of wisdom to the focused mind. In a letter to Pope Gregory the Great requesting an audience, the Celtic cleric Columban of Luxeuil wrote, "I do want to see you, that I might drink in that spiritual stream of living water of knowledge." Throughout Celtic Europe, water—especially when found in slow-flowing streams and deep, still pools—was believed to inspire religious contemplation and facilitate inner vision.

WELLS OF WISDOM

Wells have been revered as channels of wisdom since at least Biblical times. It was at Jacob's Well in Sychar (modern-day

Jacob's Well, Sychar

Nablus) where Jesus met a Samaritan woman and asked her to give him a drink of water. He went on to say: "Everyone who drinks of this water will thirst again, but whoever drinks of the water that I shall give will never thirst; the water I shall give him will become in him a spring of water welling up to eternal life." (John 4:13–14). In addition to documenting Jesus' revelation that he is the Messiah (John 4:25–26), their conversation touches on important issues concerning religious observance and the promise of a direct spiritual relationship with God to worship "in spirit and truth."

Wells were symbolic of grace and wisdom among peoples of many cultures. Among the Norse, wells were considered the abodes of various deities that had both the ability to heal and provide good fortune for those who respected their watery domain. The belief in well wisdom probably dates to the Tree of Yggdrasil of Eddic myth, which grew above a well of knowledge flowing from beneath its roots. The well is said to have been connected to Mimir, a water spirit, who drank of the well from the Gjallar-horn and thus possessed the wisdom of the sacred well itself.

Throughout Celtic Europe, sacred wells were considered sources of both practical knowledge and divine wisdom with the ability to teach humanity about the mysteries of life. Many such wells were identified by the presence of hazelnut trees planted nearby, because the hazelnut was a Celtic symbol of wisdom. However, those who approached the wells needed to follow strict rules of conduct, or they could be severely punished by the resident deities.

A popular Irish myth described the goddess Sinend, who visited Connla's Well (also known as the Well of Segais) located under the sea in Fairyland. The enchanted well was surrounded with hazelnut trees. When ripe, the hazelnuts would fall into the well and turn the water into a rich shade of purple. Venturing to the well in search of wisdom, the hapless goddess omitted certain preparatory rites, thus angering the resident deities. They caused the waters of the well to overwhelm Sinend and wash her body onto the shore of the Shannon—giving the river its name.

Considered the ultimate source of otherworldly wisdom by the Irish, the Well of Segais was also believed to be the source of the River Boyne. In one Celtic legend, King Cormac visited this sacred well, which was described like this: "A shining fountain, with five streams [symbolizing the five senses giving knowledge] flowing out of it, and the hosts in turn drinking its water. Nine hazels of Buan [Boand] grew over the well. The purple hazels dropped their nuts into the fountain, and five salmon which were in the fountain severed them and set their husks floating down the streams."

Another legend described a secret well of wisdom that was located in a meadow near a settlement called Sid Nechtain. Attempting to test its powers, Boanna, the wife of Nechtain, tried to prove her chastity after having an adulterous affair with Dagda the Good, the supreme head of the people of Dana.

After walking around the well the prescribed three times, "three waves from the well mutilated her, she fled, and was drowned in the pursuing waters."

WATER, MAGIC AND MIRACLES

In the Bible, water miracles exemplify the wisdom and power of God. The Old Testament describes several water-related wonders that Moses was ordered to perform, including taking water from the Nile and turning it into blood (Exodus 4:9) and dividing the waters of the Red Sea, thus allowing the people of Israel to escape from Egypt (Exodus 14:21): "Then Moses stretched our his hand over the sea; and the Lord drove

The Spring of Moses in the Sinai

the sea back by a strong east wind all night, and made the sea dry land, and the waters were divided." In Numbers 20:11, Moses created a spring of fresh water in the Sinai desert by casting his rod into the rock: "And Moses lifted up his hand and struck the rock with his rod twice; and water came forth abundantly, and the congregation drank and their cattle." (The old photograph shows the so-called Spring of Moses in the Sinai.)

Several miracles related to water are attributed to Jesus. After the multiplication of loaves and fishes and the feeding of the 5,000 described in the Gospels of Mark, Matthew, Luke, and John, his disciples were struggling to row a boat far away from shore on the Sea of Galilee and were buffeted by heavy winds. In the Gospel of John (6:16–21), Jesus left the shore and walked on the water's surface to meet their boat, revealing Jesus' mastery over the elements as the true Son of God.

John also tells us that after the crucifixion and resurrection, Jesus' disciples were fishing on the Sea of Galilee, without much success. Jesus appeared on shore and asked the men if they had caught anything. Upon hearing their negative reply, Jesus instructed his disciples to throw their net over the starboard side of the boat: They caught so many fish that it was impossible to retrieve their catch. It was also at this time that Jesus told Peter, the former fisherman, to become a "fisher of people" and to spread the Gospel throughout the world (21:1–14).

ORACLES AND DIVINATION

According to *The Encyclopedia of Religion,* oracles provide a divine pronouncement or response concerning the future—an oracle also is a place where such pronouncements are given. Throughout history, water has played an important role in oracles. In ancient Greece, water nymphs were credited with the gift of prophesy, due partly to the belief that drinking certain waters produced a state of spiritual receptivity. The Greeks also believed that Gaia, the primal earth goddess, was the source of oracular inspiration who spoke through sacred springs, pools, and trees. Water was intimately connected to Apollo's famous oracle at Delphi; although Pythia, the priestess and messenger of the oracle, was said to inhale a mysterious vapor issuing from a cleft in the rocks, she prepared for the consultations by drinking water from the sacred Kassotis spring. Water from springs was also imbibed by the priest-prophets at Apollo's oracles at Claros and Colophon, as well as the healing oracles of Demeter at Patrae and Amphilochos in Cilicia.

Among the early Jews, the diviner would fill a cup with water or wine and gaze intently at the surface, which would reputedly reveal different images for interpretation. In order to learn whether a person would survive the year, the fortune teller would draw water from a well on the eve of *Hosha'anah Rabba,* pour it into a clear glass, and place the glass in the middle of a room under the light of the moon. If a human face appeared in the water with an open mouth, the person would survive; if the mouth was closed, the hapless individual would die. Cuplike bowls glazed with magical inscriptions were filled with water and used to detect crimes, determine whether or not a woman was committing adultery, and to provide a seeker with insight into the future.

Divination from wells was an important part of Celtic everyday life. Dreaming at the water's edge was considered an effective form of divination. Young women would drink from a well and fall asleep, each in the hope of dreaming about a possible suitor as her future husband. St. Agnes's Well in Somerset, England, was a famous wishing well that was believed to possess the magical ability to bring lovers together. St. Agnes's Eve was traditionally one for love divination, and young women would assemble at the well, whispering their desires for a husband to St. Agnes. One charming legend tells about a poor woman who worked on a farm; she was skinny and not particularly beautiful and was approaching middle age. She desperately wanted children but was unable to find the appropriate husband. Upon arriving at the well on St. Agnes's Eve, she felt intimidated by all of the younger, more beautiful women who were already there, knowing that St. Agnes would grant a husband to only one of them. However, Providence shined on this woman, because a rather shy, older, but upstanding bachelor happened to be walking by that very evening. According to the tale, the two fell in love on the spot and married soon after, and "in a year or two she'd a babe in the cradle and one under her apron, and two clinging to her skirts, and they was all so happy as daisies in the sunshine."

Certain wells were regularly consulted to help determine if lovers and prospective mates were faithful, how long a person would live, and if (and when) those suffering from disease would recover from their afflictions. In consulting the well about the sick, the most common procedure was similar to that used to determining guilt or innocence of someone charged with a crime: a piece of the person's clothing would be placed on the surface of the well. If it floated, the individual would recover; and if it sank, death would inevitably follow.

The presence of fish or eels in a sacred well was considered a good omen among the Welsh during the Middle Ages because they believed that anything living in the well possessed oracular powers. In the Ffynnon Gybi Well, the patient would stand bare legged in its shallow waters; if the resident eel coiled its body around the person's leg, a cure would result. The trout living in a well called Ffynnon Beris was especially revered; if it appeared while a sick person bathed in the well, the patient's recovery would surely result. People also ventured to the well to inquire about the future and tossed a piece of bread into the water. If the fish appeared, good fortune would result; if not, the omen was unfavorable.

TAROT SYMBOLISM

The origin of Tarot cards is believed to go back many hundreds of years. Some think that the Tarot can even be traced back to ancient Egypt and Israel because of parallels that might exist between the Major Arcana and the Kabbalistic meaning of the 22 letters of the Hebrew alphabet. Others feel that the cards might be of Indian origin, because they seem to relate to many early Hindu deities.

Whatever its origin, the Tarot is regarded by many not only as an ancient source of divination, but also as a wisdom tool for self-transformation. According to Arthur Edward Waite, who developed a popular tarot deck known as the Rider-Waite Tarot, the cards embody symbolic presentations of universal ideas that lie imbedded in the consciousness of humanity. Possessing both exoteric information appropriate for the general public and more hidden meanings reserved for advanced students of esoteric philosophy, each card offers a degree of wisdom concurrent with the learner's level of understanding and degree of spiritual development.

The Star

Two cards in particular reveal wisdom provided by water symbolism. *The Star* features a naked female figure kneeling on the shore of a tranquil pool. Her left knee is on the land while her right foot is placed on the water. In her hands, the woman holds two ewers (large water jugs) that provide living nourishment to both land and sea.

According to Waite, the figure represents the Great Mother who

ACE ♦ CUPS.

The Ace of Cups

possesses supreme understanding. The card itself communicates the substance of the heavens as well as the elements of Earth, revealing the dual messages, "Waters of Life Freely" and "Gifts of the Spirit."

While all cards of the suit of cups represent the water element, the *Ace of Cups* is considered the most fortunate card to draw from the deck, because it represents joy, abundance, and fertility. The hand reaches out from a cloud, revealing its Divine origins; the image is reinforced by the dove bearing a cross-marked wafer, a sign of the Holy Spirit. The waters of life fall from the cup on all sides, both in the form of cascades of water and droplets of morning dew, onto a bed of water lilies, the ancient symbol of spiritual enlightenment.

RIVERS OF WISDOM IN INDIA AND TIBET

Every 12 years, millions of Hindus descend on the city of Allahabad to celebrate *Maha Kumbh Mela*, or Great Kumba Fair, a spectacular six-week religious festival believed to be the largest single human gathering anywhere. The core of the festival takes place at the critical junction where the sacred Ganges and Yamuna rivers converge. In the celestial realms, these rivers are joined by the mythical river Saraswati, symbol of divine knowledge. In addition to ritual bathing, the pilgrims see the numerous gurus, mystics, yogis, and other holy people who venture to Kumbh Mela offering spiritual guidance and instruction. Smaller Kumbh Melas take place at the holy cities of Nasik, Ujjain and Hardwar.

The Sanskrit word *kumbha* means "pot" and refers to a vessel containing the elixir of immortality that fell to Earth during a mythical struggle between gods and demons many thousands of years ago; the kumbha is also said to contain the essence of Brahma (the Creator), Vishnu (the Sustainer), and Shiva (the Destroyer), along with all goddesses, Mother Earth (and her seven islands), and all knowledge in the form of the *Rigveda, Yajur-Veda, Sama-Veda, and Atharva-Veda.* For this reason, Kumbh Mela is not only a festival of the story of creation but also a celebration of divine knowledge that can liberate humanity from the cycle of birth, death, and rebirth. It also provides a special opportunity to deposit the ashes of departed ancestors into the holy river in order to merge their physical remains with the maximum level of purity and Divine Wisdom that the waters represent at this time. During this sacred time, offerings to the gods often include fashioning a small boat out of aluminum foil or thatched palm leaves and filling it with coconut, marigolds, incense, and coins before prayerfully launching it into the river's currents.

The most recent Maha Kumbh Mela took place in January and February of 2001 and attracted more than 30 million participants. For many, bathing in the rivers can be a spiritual high point in their lives. In the words of one seventy-two-year-old pilgrim who attended Kumbh Mela 2001: "How a bath makes one feel is beyond words, beyond even thought. The water flows through you; the water surrounds you. But that doesn't even explain it. It's beyond explaining."

Mount Kailas lies hidden at the western end of the Great Himalayas in Tibet, its four sides facing north, south, east, and west, with a sacred river flowing from each. Both in myth and geography, the rivers are connected to Kailas, considered by both Buddhists and Hindus as the most sacred mountain on Earth and a key pilgrimage site. Known also as simply Paradisaic Abode, Mount Kailas, or Kangrinpoche, is revered by Tibetan Buddhists as the highest center of consciousness and the metaphysical center of the entire planet. For Hindus, the mountain, also known as Meru, is the abode of Shiva, where the waters of heaven pass through the god's matted hair and become healing streams.

According to Lama Anagarika Govinda, the rivers pay homage to the gods by encircling Mount Kailas seven times before beginning their outward flow. The rivers represent individual sacred animals that are throne symbols to four of the Dhyana-Buddhas. They include the sacred Brahmaputra, or *Tamchog-Khambab* (the river flowing out of the horse's mouth), the Sutlej, or *Langchen-Khambab* (the river flowing out of the elephant's mouth), the Indus, or *Senge-Khambab* (the river flowing out of the lion's mouth), and the Karnali, or *Magcha-Khambab* (the river flowing out of the peacock's mouth), a tributary of the holy Ganges.

Brahmaputra *by Nicholas Roerich (1945)*

Tibet's holiest lake, Lake Manasarovar, lies 20 miles south of Mount Kailas and is revered as a source of intense psychic energy; in fact, Hindus believe that Brahma himself (the supreme and unrecognizable Principle of the Universe from the essence of which all emanates) created Manasarovar and planted the mythical Tree of Life at its center, transforming the water into a life-giving elixir.

According to W. Y. Evans-Wentz, only the most devoted and courageous pilgrims who venture to the holy mountain and its sacred bodies of water are rewarded by an inexplicable feeling of bliss and enter into a state of cosmic consciousness: "Their mental faculties seem to be heightened, their receptivity infinitely increased, so that many see wonderful visions, and hear strange voices, and fall into a trancelike state wherein

instantaneously, as in a flash of lightning, which suddenly illu-
minates what before had been shrouded in darkness, their
impediments and difficulties disappear."

HOLY ISLANDS

Islands have always inspired awe and wonder. In contrast to the
sea, which exists in a dynamic state of constant flux, islands
offer the promise of safety, stability, and eternity. Often appearing as magical bodies floating serenely on the water's surface,
they have long been the subject of myth and legend, from King
Arthur's enchanted island of Avalon and the mythical Atlantis
to the revered Turtle Island of the Iroquois. Storm-battered
islands off the coasts of Brittany, Ireland, and Britain settled by
early Christian hermits and monks, such as Mont St. Michel,
Great Skellig, and Lindisfarne, continue to inspire visions of
mystery and ancient religious practice. Today, many islands
around the world—including remote Easter Island (Rapa Nui),
the Egyptian island of Philae (located in the middle of the
Nile), and the Scottish holy island of Iona (which became a
stronghold of Celtic Christianity in the early Middle Ages)—
remain sources of wisdom and spiritual discovery.

Thanks to their relative isolation, many islands, like the
Galápagos off the coast of Ecuador, Lomboc near Sumatra, or
some of the San Juan Islands in Puget Sound (Washington
State), have so far been able to preserve their unique ecosystems.
According to Richard Bangs, "…islands have been sanctuaries

from the ravages of Man and his ambitious works. While the great rivers of the continents have been dammed and the cities smothered in their own pollution, the relative isolation and size of islands have often left them alone with sometimes singular ecologies, and a degree of environmental, cultural and spiritual integrity."

Islands have long been important destinations for pilgrims in search of wisdom and divine grace. As mentioned earlier, a pilgrim's way circles the Japanese island of Shikoku and leads to 88 temples in a journey of more than 900 miles. The temples perch atop the mountains or overlook the sea. Pilgrims symbolically travel the path Kobo Daishi, the Buddhist saint (774–835 C.E.), trod to enlightenment. They dress as the saint, in the guise of a wandering monk, and wear white, the color of purity and death in Japan. A completed pilgrimage symbolizes rebirth and renewal. As the route circles the island, pilgrims return to the point where they started. In reality there is no final destination and many make a second and third journey. Some return hundreds of times or even walk permanently round Shikoku.

The remote island of Lindisfarne—or Holy Island— located off the Northumberland Coast, is considered one of the most inspiring pilgrimage sites in the British Isles. Missionaries from Iona established a community here in around 630 C.E. when King Oswald of Northumbria invited them to teach his people the Christian faith. Aidan, the first abbot, and his followers worked as missionaries through much of England and

Scotland and inspired many converts to return with them to the monastery for prayer and study. Soon an important center of Celtic Christianity, Lindisfarne was also renowned for its art: A splendid illuminated Latin manuscript known as the Lindisfarne Gospels was written here before 700 C.E. Today, this rocky island remains not only as a sacred pilgrimage site for those visiting the ruins of the priory and castle, but also as an important wildlife sanctuary, especially for birds.

Mount Athos forms the tip of a finger of land that juts into the sea east of Salonika in northern Greece. For almost two millennia the peninsula has been revered as the sacred territory of the Virgin Mary, and twenty monasteries of the various Christian Orthodox faiths—Greek, Russian, Serbian, and Bulgarian—are spread along its shores and among its wild mountains. Because the border between the mainland and the autonomous theocratic community of the monks prevents access by land, the only way in is by ship. Some 1,500 monks live there now—women and "beardless boys" have been forbidden access to the Holy Mountain for centuries. Pilgrims are usually permitted to stay for four days, although some are able to extend their visit. The annual procession to the top of Mount Athos begins on August 18 at the Megistis Lavra monastery and concludes with a predawn ascent to the summit for a feast day liturgy the following day.

Whether we choose to visit a sacred pilgrimage site or simply take a quiet walk along a river, a lake, or the ocean, we can strive to experience nature directly. Energetic resonance with bodies of water can provide us with the natural wisdom that so many of us yearn to rediscover. Through greater intimacy with the natural world, we begin to appreciate its complexity and gain a clearer understanding of the relationship between the rains, the soil, and the plants, the animals and the trees, and how the welfare of one living being depends on that of another.

9

ENCHANTMENT

*The great sea has sent me adrift. It moves me as
the weed in a great river. Earth and the great
weather move me. Have carried me away. And
move my inward parts with joy.*

—UVAVNUK, INUIT HOLY WOMAN

Humans have been enchanted by water since our earliest history. Water has moved us, and left us delighted, surprised, and transformed. Water has inspired the vision of philosophers, musicians, religious leaders, poets, and artists. The sensitive, dreamlike renderings of waterfalls and lakes by Chinese artists are legendary, as are the powerful depictions of water by Japanese artists such as Utagawa Hiroshige and Katsushika Hokusai, whose woodblock print *Beneath the*

Beneath the Wave off Kanagawa *by Katsushika Hokusai (1827)*

Wave off Kanagawa, created in 1827, is perhaps Japan's most celebrated work of graphic art. The luminous paintings of water by the American artists Albert Bierstadt, George Catlin, Thomas Cole, Frederick Church, and other members of the Hudson River School of Painting reveal an almost supernatural connection with water that goes beyond the traditional five senses. The literary works of Henry David Thoreau, Ralph Waldo Emerson, Walt Whitman, John Muir, Thomas Berry, and others also reveal an intimate connection with, and an unusual awareness and a sensitivity to, water. In the final stanza of his poem "Fog," Thoreau wrote:

> Spirit of lakes and rivers—seas and rills
> Come to revisit now thy native scenes

Night thoughts of earth—dream drapery
Dew cloth—and fairy napkin
Thou wind-blown meadow of the air.

Inherent in the quality of enchantment is the adventure of being connected with the movement of life and the joy of being at one with nature. Walking along a beach, the bare feet wet from the ocean surf, feeling the spray of a crashing waterfall, or swimming in the cool waters of a mountain lake can create lasting memories. During his epic journey to Asia, the Italian explorer Marco Polo visited West Lake, near the ancient Chinese city of Huangzou. After his hosts took him on an excursion on this sacred lake, believed to have been created by a dragon and a phoenix, he declared, "A voyage on this lake offers more refreshment than any other experience on Earth."

Water can provide a powerful contrast to the bustle of a large city, as visitors to Manhattan's Riverside Park or Chicago's Grant Park can attest. One of the most enchanting watery places to visit in the United States is the celebrated Riverwalk, or Paseo del Rio, in San Antonio, Texas. Meandering through downtown, the tree-lined San Antonio River is spanned by many pedestrian bridges; its banks are occupied by restaurants, coffee shops, hotels, and retail stores. Flat-bottomed boats carry passengers leisurely along the river, which provides both tranquillity and a cool respite from the often hot streets above.

Ice and snow offer their own brand of enchantment. Walking in the forest or through a park after a heavy snowfall

Montmorency Falls, near Québec City

transforms an often familiar environment into a new and wondrous world of light and form. Winter activities such as ice skating, cross-country skiing, snow shoeing, sledding, and tobogganing provide a unique combination of excitement and sense of beauty and "connectedness" with the natural world, as illustrated by an early lithograph of the winter scene at the Montmorency Falls near Québec City, Québec.

BEAUTY

Throughout human history, beauty has been an essential component in spiritual understanding. To the Navajo, for example, beauty has always been recognized as the culmination of the subtle intelligent life of the universe. Natural forms such as mountains, rivers, lakes, and springs are all considered to be the homes of powerful spirit beings.

Waterfalls have a special ability to make us aware of the beauty of water; we are impressed and moved as we watch many thousands of gallons of water descending rapidly over the edge and cascading into a pool or crashing onto rocks below. In *The Meaning of Shinto*, J. W. T. Mason captures the essence of a sacred waterfall with awe and reverence:

> The Nachi Waterfall descends from a great height amid graceful, bowing foliage. The spray softly strokes the rocks and disappears into invisibility while the trees stand guard against pollution. The water follows its narrow downward way gently, with swift, smooth unconscious accuracy seeking its spreading goal beneath. The white threads of the falling current seem like ethereal coverings

Niagara Falls

Beaver Meadow Falls, Lake Placid, New York

of purity, enveloping an inner spiritual power emerging
from lofty Heaven into the universe beyond.

The sound of falling water often touches us emotionally as
well, be it a deep roar like that found at Niagara Falls or the
joyous splashing of a waterfall like Beaver Meadow Falls in the
Adirondack Mountains near Lake Placid.

In *The World Is as You Dream It,* about his experiences with
the Shuar people of Ecuador, John Perkins writes movingly of
the transformative beauty of a sacred waterfall:

The sacred waterfall of the Shuar is breathtaking and
beautiful. Yet standing before it, looking up into the rainbow that arches through the cascading waters, the visitor

is struck by a feeling that transcends the magnificence of the landscape. No matter what your religion, you cannot help but sense the spirit of this place. Its power defies any attempt to describe the euphoria inspired by a natural phenomenon so overwhelmingly grand that its voice seems to cross all the bridges of time, speaking to us from some ancient past as well as from the unknown future.

Like waterfalls, the ocean possesses an ever-changing beauty that varies not only with the time of day but also with the constant changes in currents, tides, wind velocity, and precipitation. Standing or sitting on the shore and simply watching the waves crashing against it offers an experience of both inspiration and beauty. Watching the sun set over the ocean is a daily ritual for many coastal dwellers and visitors, such as

Big waves at Santa Barbara, California

those who come together at Mallory Pier in Key West, Florida, to watch an often dazzling subtropical sunset. As the sun disappears below the horizon, it is often acknowledged by sustained applause from the crowd.

RAINBOWS

As one of Earth's most magical images, the rainbow, with its graceful bands of luminous color, has endured as a symbol in myth and legend for millennia. For many today, the rainbow has become a symbol of achieving unity through diversity and especially of the quest to understand divergent points of view.

A rainbow is created when light interacts with water droplets; the sun must be behind the droplets with respect to the observer. A beam of white sunlight enters the raindrops and refracts at the front surface of the drops, producing a complete spectrum of colors. With a large group of droplets, different colors will appear according to the color spectrum: red will appear on top of the rainbow, green will be in the middle, and blue or violet on the bottom.

Until René Descartes scientifically analyzed the formation of rainbows in the seventeenth century, their origin was shrouded in superstition. An ancient Chaldean story describes how the goddess Ishtar lifted up a mighty bow after the flood, and a Greek legend tells how Aphrodite, wounded in battle, escaped to Olympus along the rainbow route carried by Iris, a granddaughter of Oceanus and a goddess of wind and rain. In the Umbanda and Candomblé faiths in Brazil, which, like Cuba's Santería, trace their roots to the Yoruba religion of what is now Nigeria, Oshunmaré is the god of rainbows and is responsible for the communication between the superior and inferior cosmic regions of existence. Traditional teachings claim that Oshunmaré represents the integration between the male and female aspects of nature whose undulating movements are like those of a snake, revealing the link between heaven and Earth.

In the West, perhaps the most powerful religious image invoked by the rainbow is that expressed in Genesis 9:13–17, revealing the benign presence of God and his covenant with humanity after the flood:

> I set my bow in the cloud, and it shall be a sign of the covenant between me and the earth. When I bring clouds over the earth and the bow is seen in the clouds, I will remember my covenant which is between me and you and every living creature of all flesh; and the waters shall never again become a flood to destroy all flesh. When the bow is in the clouds, I will look upon it and remember the everlasting covenant between God and every living creature of all flesh that is upon the earth.

To this day, when a religious Jew sees a rainbow, he or she will often say the following blessing: "Blessed art thou, the Eternal, our God, King of the Universe, who remembereth the covenant, is faithful thereto, and adhereth to his word." A

related Celtic belief held that the presence of a rainbow during a year is a sign that the world will not come to an end
within the next 40 years: "So the rainbow appear, the world
hath no fear, until thereafter forty year."

Although the appearance of a rainbow today is almost
always considered a sign of good fortune in the West—personified by the popular belief that a pot of gold can be found
at its base—earlier peoples harbored decidedly ambivalent feelings about them. While most European peoples believed that a
rainbow appearing at the birth of a child was a sign of good
fortune, the Slavs feared that it foretold the baby's eventual illness and death. In parts of Europe it was believed that if the
base of the rainbow touched land, good fortune would ensue,
but if it touched water, bad fortune would eventually come
about. These mixed feelings often found expression in rhymes
and sayings, some based on local observations by farmers and
other people who lived on the land, such as "Rainbow at night,
shepherd's delight; rainbow in morning, shepherds take warn-
ing," or "If there be a rainbow in the eve, it will rain and leave,
but if there be a rainbow in the morrow, it will neither lend nor
borrow."

Others cultures perceived rainbows as essentially negative.
In parts of Africa, for example, the rainbow was viewed as a
giant serpent that would emerge after a rain to graze. Anyone
coming too close to the rainbow would be drowned, and the
inhabitants of a home that was touched by the base of the
rainbow were certain to suffer illness and other misfortune.

CELEBRATION: WATER FESTIVALS AND HOLIDAYS

Humanity has been celebrating water festivals for thousands of years. One of the biggest bathing festivals is *Maghi Purnima* in India, known for its piety and devotion. Celebrated on the full moon day of Magha (which falls either in late January or early February), literally millions of devotees, including pilgrims, ascetics, mendicants, priests, and yogis, venture to designated spots along the sacred Ganges, Yamuna, Surayu, Narmada, and Tapti rivers for a sacred bath, while others often walk for many miles to bathe in the ocean, a lake, or a holy tank. One such tank, the Kumbhakonam near the city of Chennai (Madras), is believed to be magically filled with Ganges water on that day.

Simhat Beit Ha-sho'evah

Water festivals traditionally are connected with calling forth the rains. One of the earliest was *Simhat Beit Ha-sho'evah,* a Jewish tradition dating back to pre-Biblical times. Also known as the Feast of Water-Drawing, it originally took place at the First Temple during the Feast of Tabernacles, also known as *Succot,* the Jewish holiday that recalls the time when the children of Israel lived in temporary dwellings in the desert after the exodus from Egypt. Succot emphasizes the notion of trusting in God's protection and the importance of being grateful. During Succot, meals are taken in temporary outdoor structures, which are also used for prayer and reflection. While Simhat Beit Ha-sho'evah differed slightly every year, it is described by Heinrich Graetz as essentially a joyous celebration:

> At times these bore a lively character, such as torch-light processions and dancing; at others they took a more solemn form of musical services of song and praise. The jubilee would last the whole night. At break of day the priests announced with a blast of their trumpets that the march was about to commence. At every halting-place the trumpets gathered the people together, until a huge multitude stood assembled at the spring of Siloah. Thence the water was drawn from a golden ewer. In solemn procession it was carried back to the Temple, where the libation was performed. The water streamed over the altar, and the notes of the flute, heard only upon the most joyous occasions, mingled with the rapturous strains of melody that burst from countless instruments.

In addition to prayers for rain, Simhat Beit Ha-sho'evah was noted for its revelry. Joyous singing, clapping, shouting, and dancing were the order of the day, and festive bonfires were set both in the Temple courtyard and outside every Jewish home in Jerusalem. It was celebrated with such enthusiasm that it led to the popular phrase, "whoever had not seen it did not know the meaning of joy." The festival ceased when the Temple was destroyed by forces under the Babylonian king,

Nebuchadnezzar, although the tradition of water-drawing continues, though to a lesser extent, at some synagogues today.

The Dragon Boat Festival

The *Dragon Boat Festival* is one of the most spectacular traditions of ancient China. Competing teams row their dragon-shaped boats to the beating of drums. More than 20 million people in mainland China, Hong Kong, Singapore, Taiwan, and Malaysia participate in this festival, making it one of the most beloved spectator sports in the world. Becoming increasingly popular in Europe and North America in recent years as well, the Dragon Boat Festival is now also celebrated in cities such

Dragon boat race, Singapore

as Ottawa, Vancouver, Victoria, Edmonton, Regina, Toronto, and Montréal in Canada, and New York City, San Diego, Portland (Oregon), and Burlington (Iowa) in the United States.

The legend behind the festival tells a story of love and devotion to one's country. Some 2,300 years ago, a poet named Qu Yuan served his government as Minister of State. Accused by rivals that he was corrupt, Qu Yuan was unable to regain the emperor's favor and on the fifth day of the fifth month of the lunar year, he threw himself into the Mei Lo River in what is now Hunan province, either in an act of despair or as a final protest against government corruption. The people who lived in the area knew Qu Yuan as an upstanding and righteous man, and local fishermen jumped into their boats to try to rescue him. In an attempt to prevent fish from eating his body, they thrashed the waters with their oars; this led to the custom of throwing bamboo leaves filled with cooked rice into the water so that the fish would symbolically eat the rice rather than the beloved poet.

The festival itself became popular during the Tang Dynasty (617–907 C.E.), and it eventually spread throughout the Yangtze Valley. One of the rowers stands in the boat symbolically searching for Qu Yuan's body; the drummer and ferocious dragon designs at the bow and stern of the boat are said to frighten away evil water spirits. As the Chinese traditionally considered dragons to be deities with powers over rainfall, this festival also became connected to an appeal for abundant rains and fertile crops.

Other water festivals in Asia call forth the rains and are times for washing away bad fortune and ensuring good health and longevity.

The Water Splashing Festival

The *Water Splashing Festival* is celebrated by the Dai people, an ethnic minority who live in Xishuangbanna and Dehong Prefectures in Yunnan province, China, where the belief in Hinayana Buddhism is strong. Held in the sixth month of the Dai calendar (usually in the middle of April), it is also known

Dai Water Festival

as the Festival for Bathing Buddha, because it is related to the Buddhist legend of a dragon sprinkling fragrant showers on the Lord Buddha when he was born.

Because the Water Splashing Festival is the most important holiday among the Dai, they celebrate it with gusto. In addition to bathing Lord Buddha, dragon boat racing, fireworks, and dancing, young men and women throw a finely embroidered purse toward the object of their affection. One part of the festival that has been described as "sprinkling water on each other for good fortune" is in fact a giant water fight where everyone ends up completely—and happily—soaked.

The Songkran Festival

The *Songkran Festival* also takes place in mid-April, during the traditional Thai New Year. Because the Thai believe that water is a spiritual cleanser that washes away bad fortune, this festival is a treasured national tradition, especially in northern Thailand. As part of the more tame aspects of this festival, small drops of water are respectfully sprinkled on elders and monks as a New Year's blessing, and Buddhist images are carefully washed with water at the temple. However, people (usually children) also hide by their houses waiting for passers-by, who are then "attacked" and thoroughly soaked with water from cups, buckets, water pistols, and hoses. In some areas, the celebration includes beauty contests and parades.

Enchantment

The Festival of Yemanjá

In Brazil, the annual homage to Yemanjá, the ocean goddess, is celebrated on New Year's Eve by followers of Umbanda and Candomblé. Yemanjá is known both in Africa and Brazil as the mother of all *orishas* (gods and goddesses of nature) and is compared to Our Lady of Conception in the Roman Catholic Church. As one of the most popular and revered orishas in Brazil, Yemanjá's domain includes the ocean and all bodies of salt water. Representing the maternal forces of nature, she is often depicted as a beautiful and exalted figure dressed in flowing white robes.

On New Year's Eve, tens of thousands of Yemanjá's disciples dress in white and descend on Brazil's many beaches—the most important being Copacabana in Rio de Janeiro. Offerings of white flowers, candles, and perfume (reputed to be vain and temperamental, Yemanjá is said to love perfume) are made and lit candles are often placed in small homemade paper boats, together with messages bearing the person's requests for the New Year, and the little boats are set adrift on the ocean. Another ritual calls for digging a hole in the sand, into which are placed the offerings; the hole should be deep enough to protect the lighted candle from being extinguished by the wind. Others walk into the ocean bearing a bouquet of white flowers (usually roses); worshippers offer a prayer and make a request to Yemanjá upon entering the water and count the number of waves that wash by. After the seventh wave, they cast the flowers into the surf to be received by the ocean goddess.

It is widely believed that after the offerings are accepted by Yemanjá, the wishes will be granted during the following year. Dancing and singing often continue throughout the night and well into New Year's Day.

Festivals of Ice and Snow

Celebrated during the coldest months of winter, these festivals are more recent creations. In northern China, the *Ice and Snow Festival* is celebrated every December 31 in the city of Harbin, the capital of Heilongjiang province. Large blocks of ice are harvested from the frozen Songhua River and are fashioned into elaborate sculptures depicting Chinese lanterns, trees, mountains, pagodas, temples, and other landmarks. The river itself has a rich mythical history. Rising from Lake Tianchi atop Mount Baitou, the water tumbles down the mountain as if falling from heaven, earning the Songhua the ancient name of Tianhe, or River from Heaven.

Perhaps the best-known Asian celebration of ice and snow is the *Sapporo Snow Festival* on the northern Japanese island of Hokkaido. Held for seven days during February, this annual event attracts some 2 million visitors from both Japan and abroad. The highlight of the festival is hundreds of beautiful snow statues and ice sculptures that line the walkways of Odori Park, the grounds of an army base in Makomanai, and the main street in Susukino. Many of the larger sculptures (which can be more than 50 feet high, 60 feet wide, and 70 feet long) are reproductions of famous landmarks in Japan and abroad, such as the Meiji Jingu shrine in Tokyo or the Blue Mosque in Istanbul.

Québec City is home to the world's oldest and largest snow and ice festival, the *Québec Winter Carnival.* Established in 1894, this ten-day extravaganza attracts a million visitors and includes the world's largest snowmobile race (a six-day trip along 3,000 kilometers of cross-country trails), a dogsled race through Québec City's snowy streets, nightly parades with costumes and floats, cross-country ski competitions, an often dangerous canoe race through the ice floes on the St. Lawrence River, igloo-building workshops, and a round of formal evening balls, to which have recently been added more rowdy

At the head of the slide, Dufferin Terrace, Québec City

all-night parties. One of the more unusual activities is the famous snow bath, where about 100 hearty individuals in swimsuits frolic in the snow. The entire festival is presided over by a jolly snowman named Bonhomme Carnaval. In addition to residing in a specially built palace made of ice or snow for the duration of the carnival, he has the happy task of crowning the Carnival Queen at the official opening of the yearly festivities. One of the most popular activities for children (and adults) is racing down the famous toboggan slide on Dufferin Terrace, located in front of the venerable Château Frontenac Hotel.

COMMUNION AND MEDITATION

Although we commune with the inner essence of water whenever we drink it or take a dip in a lake or stream, few of us do so with awareness. No matter what your religious or cultural background might be, a greater sensitivity and respect for water can enrich your everyday life.

When we turn on the tap, for example, we can express gratitude for the gift of water; as we water the plants on our window-sill or in our garden, we can envision how the water traveled all the way from its source to become nourishment; and when a heavy rainfall catches us without an umbrella, we can try not to get upset but acknowledge that our survival is dependent on it.

Many pleasurable water-related activities can deepen our spiritual connection to water. Swimming in the ocean, standing under a rushing waterfall, snorkeling above multicolored coral reefs, walking along the bank of a river, taking a canoe out on a lake in the early morning, or observing the sun as it sets over the ocean are just some of the activities that can increase our physical and spiritual connection to the water element in nature.

Even taking a warm bath can be a way of reconnecting to our bodies and communing with water. In *Lit from Within: Tending the Soul for Lifelong Beauty,* Victoria Moran devotes an entire chapter to the Saturday Night Bath and explores how we can experience the pleasurable nurturing of the water, no matter how thin or beautiful our bodies may or may not appear: "In order to take a bath, you can't help but acknowledge that your body is there. When it's being caressed by the heavenly warmth, you and your body share the pleasure."

Like a bath, a morning shower can take on new meaning if we consciously choose to view it as a spiritual experience. When we turn on the water, we can say a quiet prayer, and ask to be cleansed of all negativity so that our hearts and spirits are pure.

Although meditation is commonly practiced indoors, meditating in nature while facing the ocean, a waterfall, lake, brook, or river can be a powerful spiritual experience. If the water is not too cold, meditating while being partially submerged in it can provide an even deeper sense of communion with the physical and spiritual energies of water as they permeate our entire

Lotus *by Nicholas Roerich (1933)*

being—as depicted in the painting of the meditating holy man by Nicholas Roerich.

There are many ways to meditate in a natural setting. The following method is but one of many and can easily be modified according to your personal needs and goals.

Find a comfortable place where you can be quiet and alone and select a comfortable position. (Some may prefer sitting in a chair, while others would rather sit in a cross-legged position on a cushion or rug.) Or, you may wish to lean against a tree or lie down on the ground.

For those who prefer to meditate with eyes open, quietly observe the body of water; if you are meditating by the ocean, you might focus your gaze at a spot about 20 to 30 feet in front of you; if you are meditating by a waterfall, you can observe the water as it begins to fall from the summit or at a point midway on the water's cascade. This will keep your mind from wandering. If you prefer to close your eyes, try to visualize a field of white light while being aware of the natural sounds around you.

Begin to breathe slowly and deeply, becoming aware of your breath as it enters and leaves your body. Each time your mind wanders to other thoughts or is disturbed by outside noises, gently bring your attention back to the easy, natural rhythm of your breathing. If you have trouble keeping your mind on your breath, count each inhalation and exhalation up to ten, and then start over again.

As you relax physically, you may find that various feelings come and go. They shouldn't be repressed, but the very act of calmly observing them may cause the images and feelings to gradually lose their intensity.

Gradually intuit and then visualize the concept of oneness with the body of water you are observing, and gradually expand your feelings of oneness to include all beings. Express your desire to experience the reality of oneness as an integral part of your life today, either in silence or out loud: "I pray to realize my connection with nature today." Repeat this visualization slowly several times. You can also express other desires or yearnings you have that you want to integrate into your life during the day. This process is akin to "sending a letter of intent to the universe."

After having expressed your keynote visualization, relax and become receptive once more. Continue your slow, deep breathing for at least three minutes and feel the sense of oneness living inside your body, near the heart. Feel it streaming out toward the body of water, and farther out into the world. End your meditation gradually and in silence.

KUAN YIN: WORKER OF MIRACLES

In the Buddhist faith, a *Botisattva* is a being who needs only one more incarnation to become a perfect Buddha. Kuan Yin, the Goddess of Compassion, is among the most important of the Botisattvas and serves as the symbol of the Divine Mother for millions. She is often depicted in deep meditation, either sitting or standing on a cloud, on a lotus blossom, or on a lotus petal floating in the sea. In some Chinese myths, Kuan Yin is sometimes portrayed as a goddess of the sea, standing or sitting serenely amid rocks and waves splashing around her feet.

Devotees who meditate upon Kuan Yin sometimes use a water visualization from the *Amitayus Sutra,* a daunting task for even the most advanced meditators. According to John Blofeld, the visualization (which is supposed to be viewed as clearly as one observes one's hand before one's eyes) includes the mental creation of 8 pools flowing into 14 channels, each displaying radiant colors and 7 precious jewels. They are also asked to visualize 600,000 lotuses in each pool, each with 7 jewels and possessing a girth 12 times the distance "covered by an army

Kuan Yin

in a day's march." Kuan Yin's height is supposed to be imagined as that same distance multiplied by the number of grains of sand found in 600,000 million rivers, with each being the length of the Ganges!

As the Buddhist counterpart to the Virgin Mary, Kuan Yin is believed to perform miracles, particularly those in response to 13 cases of calamities, or stresses, in which devotees pray for her compassionate intervention. Because Kuan Yin is so closely connected to the water element, several of her miracles involve water. Some of these calamities are described by Diana Y. Paul: "Fire is the first calamity, which will change into a cool pond when Kuan-Yin's name is invoked. During floods, the second calamity, safety will be assured for those who worship the

Botisattva. The sailor who sets out on the high seas in search of fortune but fearful of shipwreck and oceanic demons has no cause for concern, for if even one sailor calls out 'Kuan-yin' the entire crew will be saved."

Those who follow Kuan Yin often believe that personal cleanliness is a reflection of spiritual purity. On the morning of the annual festival to celebrate her assumption to Botisattvahood, temples devoted to Kuan Yin are swept and scrubbed until they are spotlessly clean. The nuns and lay people who join the monks also take a ritual bath before they participate in the festival.

10

PROTECTING
THE WATERS

Water is both a necessity of life and a
sacred symbol upholding life.
—POPE JOHN PAUL II

Paradoxically, at the same time that destruction of Earth's ecosystems poses an ever-increasing threat to the survival of all living things, environmental awareness is also very high. Most of us are conscious of the devastating consequences of deforestation, overindustrialization, and pollution of our precious natural resources. We know that pure air, clean water, and healthy trees are natural treasures that must be preserved and protected in order to sustain and nurture future generations.

Yet while there is the ever-growing awareness of the

threats to the biosphere of which we are a part, many of us remain more committed to the *idea* of protecting the environment than to its *substance*. If we want our planet to survive, we need to make a far greater personal commitment to protecting the Earth—and especially its vulnerable water environment—than we have in the past. According to His Holiness Tenzin Gyatso, the fourteenth Dalai Lama, "It is not difficult to forgive destruction in the past which resulted from ignorance. Today, however, we have access to more information, and it is essential that we re-examine ethically what we have inherited, what we are responsible for, and what we will pass to coming generations."

Any act of protection—from using less water at home to providing money to an organization involved in preserving a river—is good and useful. Yet when based on a deeper personal understanding and appreciation of water, each outward act takes on added significance and power. We need to become planetary stewards dedicating our lives to saving the precious waters of the Earth that sustain and nurture us in so many ways. At this critical period in human and planetary history, the Earth's survival is endangered by pollution, the destruction of forests, the loss of numerous plant and animal species, the disappearance of the ozone layer, and global warming, just to name a few of the major threats. Thus each of us is called upon to become—to the best of our ability—an enlightened, compassionate, and nurturing human being dedicated to protecting and preserving our planetary home in any way possible.

In an early Hebrew text, Ecclesiastes Rabbah 7:28, we read: "In the hour when the Holy One created the first human being, God took the person before all the trees of the garden of Eden, and said to the person: 'See my works, how fine and excellent they are! Now all that I have created, for you I have created. Think upon this, and do not corrupt and desolate my world; for if you corrupt it, there is no one to set it right after you.'" We have received innumerable blessings from Earth that sustain us and nurture us in a myriad of ways. Yet the task of protecting these gifts is ours alone, by working in cooperation with nature.

Humility plays an essential role in teaching us about life, and allows us to focus on what is truly important. Through destructive events such as earthquakes, tidal waves, hurricanes, droughts, and floods, nature is a powerful teacher of humility. These events often leave lasting and devastating impressions on those of us who have witnessed them first hand and force all of us to reflect on humanity's role in contributing to their severity. For example, much of the terrible destruction brought about by the extensive 1999 flooding in northern Venezuela originated, at least in part, in the clear-cutting of tropical forests for cattle grazing, wood pulp, and urbanization. The complex root systems of trees and other tropical plants are designed to absorb the moisture from rains and preserve the integrity of the soil. Without these natural regulators, the depleted soil is unable to contain the rains. Uncontrolled flooding results, with often devastating consequences.

As was mentioned in Chapter 2, other disasters are due to choosing locations for homes and businesses that do not respect the natural features of the land. The practice of building houses on sand dunes overlooking the sea often ignore the ocean's natural cycles of beach erosion and replenishment, whereas locating farms on flood plains ignores a river's seasonal rhythms of ebb and flow. The severity of floods is often increased by our attempts to control the natural movement of rivers with levees, dams, and dikes; in addition, these barriers often destroy the habitats of indigenous animals, insects, and plants. Dams can eliminate entire human communities as well; the controversial Three Gorges Dam on the sacred Yangtze River in China is expected to force the relocation of some

Wuxia Gorge of the Three Gorges of the Yangtze River

7 million people, and its huge reservoir will inundate thousands of temples, shrines, and other holy sites.

When a powerful storm hits, the waterways can overwhelm their artificial confines, causing severe flooding. Hydrologists are now devising ways to help minimize uncontrolled flooding by encouraging the planting of trees, restoring rivers to their natural channels, and advising people to relocate their farms, homes, and businesses on higher ground.

The huge Glen Canyon Dam on the Colorado River, completed in 1963, created Lake Powell, a desert pleasure pond that ranks as the second-largest manmade lake in the United States. The near-breaching of the dam by heavy rains in 1983 is believed to have compromised the integrity of its sandstone spillways; had they cracked, tremendous flooding could have destroyed at least one of the six other dams located downstream. By 2000, an unlikely alliance of scientists and environmentalists suggested that the benefits of the dam were not worth its cost, and called for Glen Canyon's gradual decommissioning. In other parts of the West, including California, Oregon, and Washington, the same argument has already led to the decommissioning of smaller dams. In early 2001, former Secretary of the Interior Bruce Babbitt observed that the movement to take dams out of service and allow rivers to reestablish their natural flow is "moving beyond preservation and protection toward . . . the affirmative act of restoration."

Decades of unlimited logging, overgrazing by livestock, faulty irrigation schemes, and depletion of precious aquifers have brought about the gradual spread of deserts in many parts of the world. In his 1993 Lenten Message, Pope John Paul II expressed his concerns about desertification directly and urgently:

> Today we are concerned to see the desert expanding to lands that only yesterday were prosperous and fertile. We cannot forget that in many cases man himself has been the cause of the barrenness of lands that have become desert, just as he has caused the pollution of formerly clean waters. When people do not respect the goods of the earth, when they abuse them, they act unjustly, even criminally, because for many of their brothers and sisters their actions result in poverty and death.

Water is essential to our survival: for drinking, washing, cleaning our homes and clothing, as well as for protecting us from fire; for use in religious ceremonies, such as ritual cleansing and purification, and for healing, initiation, and in gaining wisdom. As the key factor in the growth of human civilizations, water has been vital for agriculture, architecture, transportation, and industry. Present in all planetary ecosystems, water is at the heart of our physical, emotional, and spiritual well-being.

Preserving and protecting the waters of the world should not be seen as an obligation or chore but should spring forth as the natural result of personal awareness and appreciation of the role water plays in our lives every single day. The noted

Latone Basin and Fountain, Park of Versailles, France

Indian teacher, J. Krishnamurti, stressed that the best form of meditation involves being choicelessly aware from moment to moment. We should become aware of water while we take our morning shower, drink a glass of it, flush the toilet, or do the laundry. We should be mindful of water whenever we use it, when we stand in awe of a spectacular fountain, quietly observe a river or stream, wade into the ocean surf, or take a walk in the rain without an umbrella. Over time, we create within ourselves a water consciousness that can have a powerful and lasting impact. Because each of us is a cell in the body of humanity, a transformation of consciousness by a relatively small group of people can, over time, have a powerful impact on the world as a whole.

CONSERVATION AT HOME

By establishing common-sense lifestyle habits that cooperate with nature's healing rhythms in our homes and local communities, we assist in planetary healing and regeneration. One of the best ways to save water in our houses or apartments is to install low-flow devices in the shower and toilet bowl; while we will have enough water to enjoy our shower or flush the toilet, we will use substantially less than before. Thanks to the use of such water-saving appliances, the residents of Tucson, Arizona, have been able to reduce their per capita consumption of water to among the lowest in the United States.

Even minor changes in personal habits can save water. By turning off the tap when we soap up in the shower, brush our teeth, or shave, we can save several extra gallons of water every day.

Some new toilet bowl designs offer a dual-action flushing system that provides additional water when needed. Rather than flushing the toilet after each use, some choose to flush after two or three visits, or whenever necessary.

Fixing a leaky faucet can prevent the waste of hundreds of gallons of water a day. Not only that—to practitioners of Feng Shui, a dripping faucet symbolizes a drain on one's personal finances, so they recommend the immediate repair of all household leaks.

Recycle gray water (see page 240). Water the garden with bath water or the water used for washing dishes (it is important to only use phosphate free, biodegradable detergents).

Many people who move to semi-arid or desert regions of the country landscape their property with water-hungry, non-native plants. By deciding to plant species that are indigenous to our local bioregion, we can save tremendous amounts of water.

For many families, a lush, green lawn is sacrosanct. Because such lawns tend to require nearly constant watering for much of the year, alternatives using native grasses and other cover plants can be explored. Planting desert gardens in places such as Arizona, Nevada, and Southern California containing cacti and other succulents are often in harmony with the native land-scape, and require very small amounts of water to sustain.

Because water is required in the manufacture of consumer goods, buying only what we really need can reduce water con-sumption dramatically. Repairing a broken appliance rather than buying a new one can reduce water waste as well.

Generating electricity impacts greatly on water resources, whether used for producing hydropower or as a coolant at nuclear power plants. By using energy-saving appliances in the home and conserving energy whenever possible, we can reduce our reliance on the world's precious water supplies.

As shown in Chapter 2, a traditional mixed western diet containing meat and dairy products utilizes an average of 2,500 gallons of water per person per day (including irrigation of feed crops, animal drinking water, sanitation, and meat pro-cessing), while a plant-based diet utilizes only a fraction of that amount. By eating less meat, we can indirectly reduce our personal consumption of water by several hundred thousand gallons a year.

NEW TRENDS IN WATER MANAGEMENT

Over the past few years, several exciting trends in the wise management of water resources have been developed that can both protect the environment and limit the waste of precious water throughout the world.

Recycling Gray Water

At least one-third of the water used in the industrialized countries of the world—which is estimated at some 50 liters per person a day—is literally flushed down the toilet. This points to the importance of utilizing "gray water" from toilets and kitchen sinks for other purposes. For example, in parts of China, gray water is routinely used in watering gardens, where plants break down and absorb pollutants (providing that the water contains only biodegradable materials). In Israel, more than 70 percent of its sewer water is treated and then used to irrigate crops; by the year 2000, some 16 percent of Israel's domestic water needs were provided by reclaimed wastewater.

Using water to flush away excrement complicates the task of managing water resources because it can overwhelm water treatment facilities and lead to unnecessary water pollution.

One practical solution is to use vacuum toilets, similar to those found on jet airliners. They use only one-half liter of water per flush, and wastes are stored in a holding tank where they can be either turned into compost or broken down anaerobically to provide bio-gas for fuel.

Local Projects for Local Conditions

In many developing nations of the world, up to one-third of the daily calorie intake, especially among rural woman and children, is burnt while obtaining water. In years past, many water projects undertaken in developing countries were based on models designed in wealthy industrialized nations; some were installed

The water carriers, San Pedro Atitlán, Guatemala

without even consulting the local people to learn about their genuine needs. As a result, many expensive and grandiose projects were found to be inappropriate for local conditions. By contrast, sensitive planners have discovered that the most successful projects involve simple technologies using local materials, such as pumpless gravitational systems, hand pumps, sand-and-gravel water purification systems, and other low-tech solutions.

Closely allied with bringing about clean water supplies in rural areas is the goal of educating the local population (ideally, involving teachers, healers, and community leaders) in personal sanitation and environmental hygiene that will help local residents protect both their families and the community's precious water supplies.

Developing New Technologies

Because they live in an often challenging desert environment, the Israelis have developed some of the most creative water-saving technologies in the world. In addition to recycling wastewater as mentioned above, they raise crops with the help of closed irrigation systems, fog-drip irrigation techniques, wind-trap funnels for moisture control, closed-cycle hydroculture (which recycles evaporated water from hothouses), and other innovative methods that use minimal moisture while recycling water as much as possible.

In California, low-pressure spraying of croplands has reduced water consumption by up to 30 percent, while laser-leveling of fields can reduce water use by up to 60 percent. In addition, planting trees reduces soil erosion, prevents desertification, and helps restore natural rain patterns. Another obvious water-saving technique that can be practiced throughout the world calls for growing less water-intensive crop varieties in arid areas.

Paying the True Cost

As mentioned earlier, governments regularly subsidize the cost of supplying water to farmers and ranchers, as well as residents of large urban areas such as Los Angeles, Las Vegas, and Phoenix, making water seem cheaper than it really is. In western areas of the United States, agribusiness and cattle ranchers pay a small fraction of the true cost of water in order to maintain their crops and animal herds, while taxpayers throughout the country pay for the difference. According to Marq de Villiers, "If we stopped subsiding water to plant water-thirsty crops alien to deserts or to irrigate pasture to raise cattle for beef (at a 50,000 to 1 ratio—1 kilo of beef from 50,000 kilos of water), if we stopped doing the wasteful things for which the American West is famous, we would have water to spare."

Critics point out that paying less than water's true monetary value encourages waste, discourages recycling, and limits the development of water-saving technologies that would save water. According to Canadian environmentalist Maurice

Strong, "If gasoline were priced to take account of its real cost, including the cost of remedying pollution, it would lead immediately to reduced consumption. So with water."

Agro-lobbyists warn that should the price of water increase, farms would fail, food prices would rise, and the urban poor would suffer. However, research has shown that when water subsidies are reduced or removed by local governments, a 10 percent price increase typically yields a reduction in water demand by 20 to 30 percent. Accountability also encourages conservation. In some Canadian cities, homeowners who pay a flat rate for water typically use an average 450 liters per person per day, whereas those who pay for the quantity they use consume an average of only 270 liters.

EXPANDING THE CIRCLE

Although we may not be able to impact global water policies directly as individuals, there is much we can do in our own communities to help preserve and protect precious water.

Knowledge is a powerful tool. In order to work effectively to protect the waters, develop a solid grounding in the basic issues of hydrology, ecology, and water use. Some of the best texts on the subject of water—along with a listing of environmental and educational organizations—are included in the Resources Section of this book.

Share your knowledge and concerns through personal contact, addressing public forums such as religious and community civic groups, and write letters to the editor of your local paper. When a local water-related issue (such as filling in a swamp or cutting down a forest to build a shopping center) comes to your attention, speak out about the environmental damage this will cause. Call on government agencies to enforce existing environmental regulations and encourage legislators to adopt new ones.

Join with your neighbors to preserve and protect wooded areas and natural marshlands, saving them from encroachment by road builders and real estate developers.

Sponsor or organize a local water festival for children that will educate them about the blessings of water and our responsibility to protect and preserve our water environment.

On a more personal level, develop a greater sensitivity toward water by visiting lakes, streams, rivers, and oceans. Get to know them more intimately through careful observation, or by creating art, taking photographs, or going for a swim. As we deepen our personal contact with these bodies of water, we often become inspired to help protect and preserve them from the deepest levels of our existence.

According to Steven C. Rockefeller, Professor of Religion at Middlebury College, "…what is needed is a commitment, so wholehearted as to be justly termed religious in quality, to a new ecological world view involving a dramatic transformation of the moral values and basic attitudes that govern life in the industrial-technological world. Only such a radical shift in values and attitudes will bring about and sustain the full range of required social changes."

His statement reflects the growing awareness that the way we treat our planetary home is an important spiritual issue, a view shared by environmentalists and religious leaders alike. Theologian Sallie McFague points out that in the past, some religious traditions have not only been centered on male dominance and male imagery for the Divine, but have also been deeply anthropocentric, focusing on human dominion over nature. Rather than viewing humans as part of the natural world and understanding that our health as a species is intimately connected to the long-term health of the environment, we have focused on the immediate welfare of humanity over all else.

At this critical time in human history, Dr. McFague calls on spiritual leaders of all faiths to analyze and re-evaluate our old anthropocentric religious views, and suggests,

> "...alternative models and metaphors to express the relation of God to the cosmos as well as the place of human beings in the cosmos" that will highlight our true role within the ecosystem, as individuals who are related in intricate ways to all others in the vast community of life. Her view addresses issues that relate to the deepest concepts of eco-spirituality, where we integrate objective scientific knowledge regarding environmental protection with spiritual sensibility.

At a time when the waters of the world are more threatened than at any previous time in human history, we need to question established dogmas that relate to the role of humanity in the natural scheme of things. By asking questions, challenging cherished beliefs, and seeking out new and more meaningful ways of viewing ourselves and the world around us, we will learn to see water in a new and different light. Rather than impose our human-centered perspectives on other forms of life, we should humbly seek to learn the ways of the natural world and appreciate its inherent sacredness. Hopefully, this eco-spiritual perspective will enable us to appreciate the importance of water as a priceless creation of the Divine that deserves our respect, reverence, and protection.

RESOURCES

RECOMMENDED READING

Life's Matrix: A Biography of Water by Philip Ball. (New York: Farrar, Strauss and Giroux, 2000). Written by a science writer and consulting editor for *Nature* magazine, it is a clear and entertaining treatise on the chemical nature of water and humanity's long relationship with it. Offers short and long-term strategies for protecting water.

Water: The Fate of Our Most Precious Resource by Marq de Villiers. (Boston: Houghton Mifflin Company, 2000). The winner of the Governor General's Literary Award for Nonfiction in Canada, this powerful and well-written book explores how water has been essential for the development of civilizations. It discusses contemporary water-use problems throughout the world and offers strategies in effective water management and environmental protection.

The Sacred Depths of Nature by Ursula Goodenough. (New York: Oxford University Press, 1998). Written by a professor of biology, this clearly written and eloquent book explores the miracle of nature, combining both modern scientific under-standing with spiritual reflection.

Spirit and Nature: Why the Environment Is a Religious Issue edited by Steven Rockefeller and John C. Elder (Boston: Beacon Press, 1992). This is an important anthology of essays by religious leaders concerning the sacredness of nature and our religious duty to protect it.

ORGANIZATIONS

American Oceans Campaign
600 Pennsylvania Avenue S.E., Suite 210
Washington, DC 20000
www.americanoceans.org

It is an organization that works to safeguard the vitality of the oceans and the coastal waters of the United States.

The Cousteau Society
870 Greenbrier Circle, Suite 402
Chesapeake, VA 23320
www.cousteau.org

Founded by Jacques Y. Cousteau, this group is dedicated to the protection and improvement of the quality of life of the water planet. Cousteau teams have explored the oceans throughout the world and their observations have been documented in numerous films and publications.

Earth Island Institute
300 Broadway, Suite 28
San Francisco, CA 94133
www.earthisland.org

This is a group that tries to "conserve, protect and restore Earth's life support systems" through education and activism. It coordinates more than 20 grassroots projects designed to saving the planetary environment.

Friends of the Earth
1025 Vermont Avenue, NE
Washington, DC 20005
www.foe.org

The world's largest environmental network, with chapters in 63 countries, is dedicated to preserving the health and diversity of the planet.

Greenpeace
702 H Street, NW
Washington, DC 20001
www.greenpeaceusa.org

As an environmental organization, it is dedicated to protecting forests, land animals, and marine life throughout the world.

International Rivers Network
1847 Berkeley Way
Berkeley, CA 94703
www.irn.org

As an educational and activist organization dedicated to halting and reversing the degradation of rivers around the world, it supports local communities working to protect their rivers and watersheds.

National Audubon Society
Living Oceans Program
700 Broadway
New York, NY 10003
www.audubon.org/campaign/lo

This is the ocean-protection campaign of an international environmental organization.

The Nature Conservancy
4245 N. Fairfax Drive, Suite 100
Arlington, VA 22201
www.nature.org

The mission of The Nature Conservancy is to preserve plants, animals, and natural communities that represent the diversity of life on Earth by protecting lands and waters they need to survive.

Seaweb

1731 Connecticut Avenue, 4th Floor

Washington, DC 20009

www.seaweb.org

This is a multimedia educational project that is dedicated to raising awareness about the ocean and the life within it.

Water Environment Federation

601 Wythe Street

Alexandria, VA 22314

www.wef.org

Founded in 1928, this is a technical and educational organization dedicated to preserving and enriching the global water environment.

NOTES

Most biblical quotes are from *The New Oxford Annotated Bible* edited by Herbert G. May and Bruce M. Metzger (New York: Oxford University Press, 1973).

I. WATER: ESSENTIAL FOR LIFE

Page 10: From Philip Ball, *Life's Matrix: A Biography of Water* (New York: Farrar, Strauss and Giroux, 1999) p. 222.

Page 11: Viktor Schauberger quoted from Callum Coats, *Living Energies* (Bath: Gateway Books, 1996) p. 107.

Page 11: From Matthew Fox, *The Coming of the Cosmic Christ* (San Francisco: Harper and Row, 1988) p. 16.

Page 13: From Charles W. Moore, *Water and Architecture* (New York: Harry N. Abrams, Inc., 1994) p. 43.

Page 14: From Frans Baartmans, *Āpah, The Sacred Water* (Delhi: B. R. Publishing Corp., 1990) p. 210.

Page 17: Information about sacred water among the Dagara from Malidoma Patrice Some, *The Healing Wisdom of Africa* (New York: Jeremy P. Tarcher/Putnam, 1998) p. 167.

Page 20: Wallum Olum quote from Lee Francis, *Native Time* (New York: St. Martins Press, 1996) p. 11.

Pages 26–27: Viktor Schauberger's views on water as a living substance from Callum Coats, *Living Energies* (Bath: Gateway Books, 1996) p. 108.

Page 34: Greek flood myth quoted from Charles Mills Gayley, *The Classic Myths in English Literature* (Boston: Ginn & Company, 1893) p. 48.

Page 35: Caddo flood myth from George A. Dorsey, *Traditions of the Caddo* (Washington: Carnegie Institute of Washington, 1905) pp. 18–19.

2: SUSTENANCE

Pages 39–40: Herodotus quoted in Klaus Lanz, *The Greenpeace Book of Water* (New York: Sterling Publishing, 1995) p. 49.

Page 41: Water areas and volume statistics from Volume 28 of the *Encyclopedia Americana* (Danbury, Conn.: Grolier, 2000) p. 434.

Page 44: Domestic Water Statistics from Thomas C. Brown, *Past and Future Freshwater Use in the United States* (Fort Collins, Colo.: U.S. Department of Agriculture, Forest Service, 1999).

Page 44: Information about leakage of water from the Delaware Tunnel from Kirk Johnson's article, "City Official Rejects Assertions that Water Supply Is in Danger," published in *New York Times,* December 9, 2000, p. B3.

Page 49: Quote regarding how rain links humanity with the divine from John S. Mbiti, *African Religions and Philosophy,* 2nd edition (Oxford: Heinemann, 1990) p. 177.

Pages 50–51: The story of Honi from Angelo S. Rappoport's *The Folklore of the Jews* (London: Soncino Press, 1937) pp. 20–21.

Pages 56–57: Information from Aaron Altschul, *Proteins: Their Chemistry and Politics* (New York: Basic Books, 1965) p. 264.

3. CIVILIZATION

Page 64: Mesopotamian well information quoted from Francis H. Chapelle, *The Hidden Sea* (Tucson, Ariz.: Geoscience Press, 1997) p. 56.

Pages 66–67: Description of the Nile's waters quoted from J. William Dawson, *Modern Science in Bible Lands* (Montreal: Dawson and Brothers, 1888) p. 322

Page 70: Ibid., p. 325.

4. SACRED SPACE

Page 91: Aaron Betsky's quote is from his article "Take Me to the Water" from *Architecture & Water,* edited by Maggie Toy (London: Academy Editions, 1995) p. 9.

Page 91: Quote about how Moroccans view water from André Paccard,

Traditional Islamic Craft in Moroccan Architecture, Vol. 2 (St. Jorioz: Editions Atelier 74, 1980) p. 491.

Page 92: Charles Moore's comments about the unifying qualities of water in architecture from his article "The Potential for Wonder" appearing in *Architecture & Water,* edited by Maggie Toy (London: Academy Editions, 1995) p. 23.

Pages 92–93: George Mitchell's quotes about moving water and pools from his book *Architecture in the Islamic World* (New York: Thames and Hudson, 1995) pp. 174 and 173, respectively.

Page 94: Charles Moore's comments about reflective water quoted from his article "The Potential for Wonder" appearing in *Architecture & Water,* edited by Maggie Toy (London: Academy Editions, 1995) p. 26.

Pages 102–3: The translation (Surya XLVII:15) is by A. J. Arberry.

Page 104: Charles Moore's quote about fountains from his book *Water and Architecture* (New York: Harry N. Abrams, Inc., 1994) p. 21.

Page 108: Yang Hing-Hsien quoted in Philippa Waring's *The Feng Shui of Gardening* (London: Souvenir Press, 1998) p. 126.

Pages 109–10: The quote from historian H. N. Wethered taken from Philippa Waring, *The Feng Shui of Gardening* (London: Souvenir Press, 1998) p. 125.

Page 112: W. S. Caine's description of the Golden Temple from his book *Picturesque India* (London: George Routledge and Sons, 1898) p. 154.

5. CLEANSING

Page 120: Robert Boyle's description of the Hudson River from his book *The Hudson River* (New York, W. W. Norton & Co., 1979) p. 16.

Page 124: Quote regarding Roman baths from Matthew Benson's *A Dictionary of the Roman Empire* (New York: Oxford University Press, 1991) p. 53.

Page 132: Quotes concerning St. Teresa's relationship with holy water from *The Life of St. Teresa of Jesus* translated by Davis Lewis (London: Thomas Baker, 1916) p. 284.

Page 132: Ibid., p. 287

Page 133: Ibid., p. 288.

Page 133: Tim Unsworth's observations about holy water from his article "Holy Waters Run Deep" in *U.S. Catholic,* February 1996, p. 50.

Page 142: Robert Medicine Grizzlybear Lake's comments about the sweat lodge from the paper, *About the Sweat Lodge and Its Use* (Discussion Committee of Pine Arbor Tribal Town, 1997), edited by Chetty Chapko.

Pages 142–43: Ibid.

Page 143: Archie Fire Lame Dear's sweat lodge observations quoted from his book *Gift of Power* (Santa Fe: Bear & Company, 1992), written with Richard Erdoes, pp. 181 and 183.

Page 144: Ibid.

6. HEALING

Page 145: George Hogben's description of healing quoted from *Spiritual Aspects of the Healing Arts,* edited by Dora Kunz (Wheaton, Ill.: Quest Books, 1985) p. 87.

Page 154: Jonas' comment regarding Luxeuil quoted from Eleanor Shipley Duckett, *The Gateway to the Middle Ages: Monasticism* (Ann Arbor: The University of Michigan Press, 1988) p. 94.

Pages 155–56: Information regarding old Japanese hot springs from Yoshio Oshima, *Thermalism in Japan* (Tokyo: The Forum on Thermalism in Japan, 1988) p. 6.

Pages 157–58: Observations about shamans and hot springs quoted from Ellen Klages's book, *Harbin Hot Springs: Healing Waters Sacred Land* (Middletown, Calif.: Harbin Springs Publishing, 1993) pp. 54–55.

Pages 160–61: Iroquois story about Nekumonta and the healing spring from *The Legends of the Iroquois,* compiled by William Canfield (Port Washington, N.Y.: Ira J. Friedman, Inc., 1971).

Pages 165–66: Quote by Dr. Robert Trotter about the Chapel Well from Francis H. Chapelle, *The Hidden Sea* (Tucson, Ariz.: Geoscience Press, 1997) p. 23.

Page 166: Creation story of the Zamzam Well from the Islamic Gateway World Wide Media Network., n.d.

Page 167: Observations on Zamzam water purity from letter titled "Makkah's Water of Benisan" by Moin Uddin Ahmed, n.d.

7. INITIATION

Page 170: Quote on John the Baptist from A. N. Wilson, *Jesus: A Life* (New York: Ballantine, 1993) p. 104

Page 173: Quote by St. Hippolitus from Kevin Orlin Johnson, *Expressions of Catholic Faith* (New York: Ballantine, 1994) p. 221.

Page 175: Information about the blessing of baptismal water quoted from *New Catholic Encyclopedia*, Vol. 5 (Washington, D.C.: Catholic University of America, 1980) p. 11.

Pages 176–77: Description of the Yao and Makua male and female initiation rites quoted from T. O. Ranger and Isario Kimambo, *The Historical Study of African Religion* (Berkeley: University of California Press, 1972) p. 237.

Page 177: Quote by the Dagara elder from Malidoma Patrice Somé's autobiography *Of Water and the Spirit* (New York: Jeremy P. Tarcher/Putnam, 1994) p. 254.

Pages 177–78: Somé's observations about the Dagara decontamination ceremony quoted from *The Healing Wisdom of Africa* (New York: Jeremy P. Tarcher/Putnam, 1998) p. 218.

Page 182: Story about the Goths of Calabria quoted from Donald A. Mackenzie, *Myths of Pre-Columbian America* (Mineola, N.Y.: Dover Publications, Inc., 1996) p. 137.

Page 183: George Catlin's description of water burial appeared in Donald Mackenzie's *Myths of Pre-Columbian America* (Mineola, N.Y.: Dover Publications, 1966) p. 130.

8. WISDOM

Page 187: St. Columban quote from Eleanor Shipley Duckett's, *The Gateway to the Middle Ages: Monasticism* (Ann Arbor: The University of Michigan Press, 1988) p. 106.

Page 189: Description of King Cormac's visit to the Well of Segais quoted from John Matthews, *The Celtic Shaman's Pack* (Shaftsbury: Element Books, 1995) p. 83.

Page 193: Story about St. Agnes' Well appeared in Katherine Briggs's *A Dictionary of British Folk-Tales in the English Language,* vol. 2 (London: Routledge and Kegan Paul, 1971) p. 342.

Page 198: Quote from celebrant at Kumbh Mela festival from Barry Bearak's article, "When Hindus Brave a Big Crush for a Little Dip," from *New York Times,* January 25, 2001, p. A10.

Pages 199–200: W. Y. Evans-Wentz observations about pilgrims venturing to Mt. Kailas quoted from his book *Cuchama and Sacred Mountains* (Athens, Ohio: Swallow Press/Ohio University Press, 1981) p. 55.

Pages 200–201: Richard Bangs's observations about islands quoted from his book, *Islandgods* (Dallas: Taylor Publishing Co., 1991) p. ix.

9. ENCHANTMENT

Pages 206–7: Thoreau's "Fog" poem from *Collected Poems of Henry Thoreau,* edited by Carl Bode (Baltimore: Johns Hopkins Press, 1965).

Pages 209–10: J. W. T. Mason's waterfall quote from his book *The Meaning of Shinto* (Port Washington, N.Y.: Kennicut Press, 1967) p. 204.

Pages 210–11: John Perkins's description of the Shuar waterfall quoted from his book, *The World Is as You Dream It* (Rochester, Vt.: Destiny Books, 1994) p. 25.

Page 216: The quote describing the Jewish "Feast of Water Drawing" from Heinrich Graetz, *History of the Jews,* Vol. 2 (Philadelphia: The Jewish Publication Society of America, 1946) p. 51.

Page 225: Victoria Moran's observations on the Saturday Night Bath quoted from her book, *Lit from Within: Tending the Soul for Lifelong Beauty* (San Francisco: HarperSanFrancisco, 2001) pp. 52–53.

Pages 229–30: Quote regarding calamities from Diana Y. Paul's *Women in Buddhism* (Berkeley: Asian Humanities Press, 1979) p. 255.

10. PROTECTING THE WATERS

Page 232: From a speech given by His Holiness, the fourteenth Dalai Lama, entitled "Peace and Environment," in recognition of World Environment Day, June 5, 1986; quoted from *Tree of Life: Buddhism and Protection of Nature* magazine, 1987.

Page 235: Secretary Bruce Babbitt's observations on the restoration of rivers quoted in Robert Sullivan's article, "River, Interrupted" *Conde Nast Traveler,* January 2001, p. 121.

Page 236: The Pope's comments regarding the threat of desertification from "John Paul's Lenten message: 'Water's sacred; protect it.'" published in *National Catholic Reporter* 29, no. 16 (19 February 1993) p. 32.

Pages 243–24: Maurice Strong's observations about gasoline and water pricing quoted in Marq de Villiers' *Water* (Boston: Houghton Mifflin Company, 2000) p. 302.

Page 243: Marq de Villiers' comments on subsiding water from his book, *Water* (Boston: Houghton Mifflin Company, 2000) p. 305.

Pages 244–45: Steven Rockefeller's quote from his article "Faith and the Community in an Ecological Age" appearing in *Spirit and Nature: Why the Environment Is a Religious Issue,* edited by Steven Rockefeller and John C. Elder (Boston: Beacon Press, 1992) p. 141.

Page 246: Sallie McFague's comments quoted from her article "A Square in the Quilt: One Theologian's Contribution to the Planetary Agenda" appearing in *Spirit and Nature: Why the Environment Is a Religious Issue,* edited by Steven Rockefeller and John C. Elder (Boston: Beacon Press, 1992) p. 57.

BIBLIOGRAPHY

1. WATER: ESSENTIAL FOR LIFE

Altman, Nathaniel. *Sacred Trees* (New York: Sterling Publishing, 2000)

Baartmans, Frans. *Apah, The Sacred Waters* (Delhi: B. R. Publishing Corporation, 1990)

Ball, Philip. *Life's Matrix: A Biography of Water* (New York: Farrar, Strauss and Giroux, 1999)

Birrell, Anne. *Chinese Mythology* (Baltimore: Johns Hopkins University Press, 1993)

Blavatsky, H. P. *Theosophical Glossary* (Los Angeles: The Theosophy Company, 1971)

Buck, Peter (Te Rangi Hiroa). *The Coming of the Maori* (Wellington: Whitcombe and Tombs, 1974)

Chapelle, Francis H. *The Hidden Sea* (Tucson, Ariz.: Geoscience Press, 1997)

Coats, Callum. *Living Energies* (Bath: Gateway Books, 1996)

Deming, H. G. *Water: The Fountain of Opportunity* (New York: Oxford University Press, 1975)

Dorsey, George A. *Traditions of the Caddo* (Washington: Carnegie Institute of Washington, 1905)

Francis, Lee. *Native Time* (New York: St. Martin's Press, 1996)

Gayley, Charles Mills, ed., *The Classic Myths in English Literature* (Boston: Ginn & Company, 1893)

Geldard, Richard G. *The Traveler's Key to Ancient Greece* (Wheaton, Ill.: Quest Books, 2000)

Gold, Peter. *Navajo & Tibetan Sacred Wisdom: The Circle of the Spirit* (Rochester, Vt.: Inner Traditions, 1994)

Graulich, Michel. *Myths of Ancient Mexico* (Norman: University of Oklahoma Press, 1997)

Haro Alvear, Silvio Luis. *El culto de agua en el reino de Quito (The Water Cult in the Kingdom of Quito)* (Quito: Instituto Ecuatoriano de Ciencias Naturales, 1974)

Hastings, James, ed., *Encyclopedia of Religion and Ethics,* Vol. 9 (New York: Charles Scribner's Sons, 1951)

Kraft, Herbert C. *The Lenape* (Newark: New Jersey Historical Society, 1986)

Lanz, Klaus. *The Greenpeace Book of Water* (New York: Sterling Publishing, 1995)

Mackenzie, Donald A. *Myths of Pre-Columbian America* (Mineola, N.Y.: Dover Publications, Inc., 1996)

McGraw-Hill Encyclopedia of Science and Technology, 8th ed., Vol. 8 (New York: McGraw-Hill Inc., 1997)

Moore, Charles W. *Water and Architecture* (New York: Harry N. Abrams, Inc., 1994)

Parrinder, Geoffrey. *African Mythology* (New York: Peter Bedrick Books, 1986)

Perkins, John. *The World Is as You Dream It* (Rochester, Vt.: Destiny Books, 1994)

Reichard, Gladys A. *Navajo Religion* (Princeton: Princeton University Press, 1977)

Schauberger, Viktor. *The Water Wizard* (Bath: Gateway Books, 1998)

Schele, Linda and David Freidel. *A Forest of Kings: The Untold Story of the Ancient Maya* (New York: William Morrow and Company, 1990)

Sejourné, Laurette. *Pensamiento y Religión en el Mexico Antiguo (Thought and Religion in Old Mexico)* (Mexico City: Fondo de Cultura Económica, 1957)

Somé, Malidoma Patrice. *The Healing Wisdom of Africa* (New York: Jeremy P. Tarcher/Putnam, 1998)

Stewart, Hilary. *Looking at Indian Art of the Northwest Coast* (Vancouver: Douglas & McIntyre, 1979)

Taylor, Colin F., ed., *Native American Myths and Legends* (London: Salamander Books, 1994)

Toy, Maggie, ed., *Architecture & Water* (London: Academy Editions, 1995)

Willoughby-Meade, G. *Chinese Ghouls and Goblins* (London: Constable & Company, 1928)

2. SUSTENANCE

Altman, Nathaniel. *Sacred Trees* (New York: Sterling Publishing, 2000)

Altschul, Aaron M. *Proteins: Their Chemistry and Politics* (New York: Basic Books, 1965)

Brown, Thomas C. *Past and Future Freshwater Use in the United States* (Fort Collins, Colo.: U.S. Department of Agriculture, Forest Service, 1999)

Chaturvedi, B. K. *Yamuna* (Delhi: Books for All, 1998)

de Villiers, Marq. *Water* (Boston: Houghton Mifflin Company, 2000)

Eliade, Mircea, ed., *The Encyclopedia of Religion,* Vol. 15 (New York: Macmillan Publishing Company, 1987)

Hastings, James, ed., *Encyclopedia of Religion and Ethics*, Vol. 4 (New York: Charles Scribner's Sons, 1951)

Johnson, Kirk. "City Official Rejects Assertions that Water Supply Is in Danger," *New York Times,* December 9, 2000

Lanz, Klaus. *The Greenpeace Book of Water* (New York: Sterling Publishing, 1995)

Laski, Vera. *Seeking Life* (Philadelphia: American Folklore Society, 1958)

Manns, Frederic. *Le symbole eau-esprit dans le judaisme ancien (The Symbol of Water-Spirit in Ancient Judaism)* (Jerusalem: Franciscan Printing Press, 1983)

Mbiti, John S. *African Religions and Philosophy*, 2nd edition (Oxford: Heinemann, 1990)

Miller, Mary and Mark Taube. *An Illustrated Dictionary of the Gods and Symbols of Ancient Mexico and the Maya* (London: Thames and Hudson, 1993)

Perlin, John. *A Forest Journey: The Role of Wood in the Development of Civilization* (Cambridge, Mass.: Harvard University Press, 1989)

Rappoport, Angelo S. *The Folklore of the Jews* (London: The Soncino Press, 1937)

Somé, Malidoma Patrice. *The Healing Wisdom of Africa* (New York: Jeremy P. Tarcher/Putnam, 1998)

Sullivan, Lawrence E. *Icanchu's Drum* (New York: Macmillan, 1988)

Watt, Bernice K., et al. *Composition of Foods* (Washington, D.C.: U.S. Department of Agriculture, 1963)

Wilford, John Noble. "New Layers of Evidence Suggest Mars Had Water," *New York Times,* December 3, 2000.

3. CIVILIZATION

Alcock, Rutherford. *The Capital of the Tycoon: A Narrative of a Three Years' Residence in Japan* (New York: Harper & Brothers, 1863)

Bettini, Sergio. *Mosaici di San Marco* (Milan: Fratelli Fabbri Editori, 1968)

Boyle, Robert H. *The Hudson River* (New York: W. W. Norton & Company, 1979)

Brangwyn, Frank and Christian Barmen. *The Bridge* (London: John Lane, The Bodley Head, 1926)

Brown, David J. *Bridges* (New York: Macmillan Publishing Co., 1993)

Dawson, J. William. *Modern Science in Bible Lands* (Montreal: Dawson and Brothers, 1888)

de Villiers, Marq. *Water* (Boston: Houghton Mifflin Company, 2000)

Gerard-Sharp, Lisa. *Insight Guide Venice* (Singapore: APA Publications, 1998)

Johnson, Kirk. "City Official Rejects Assertions that Water Supply Is in Danger," *New York Times,* December 9, 2000

Mayor, Federico. "Water and Civilization" (Commentary) *UNESCO Courier,* October 1997.

New Catholic Encyclopedia, Vol. 14 (Washington, D.C.: Catholic University of America, 1980)

Oliver, Paul, ed., *Vernacular Architecture of the World,* Vol. I (Cambridge: Cambridge University Press, 1997)

Peake, Harold and Herbert Fleure. *Peasants & Potters* (Oxford: Oxford University Press, 1927)

Smith, E. Baldwin. *Egyptian Architecture as Cultural Expression* (New York: D. Appleton—Century Company, 1938)

Strayer, Joseph, ed., *Dictionary of the Middle Ages*, Vol. 12 (New York: Charles Scribner's Sons, 1989)

4. SACRED SPACE

Braunfels, Wolfgang. *Monasteries of Western Europe* (Princeton: Princeton University Press, 1972)

Burrell, C. Colston, ed., *The Natural Water Garden* (Brooklyn: The Brooklyn Botanic Garden, 1997)

Caine, W. S. *Picturesque India* (London: George Routledge and Sons, 1898)

Cheng, Liyao. *Imperial Gardens* (New York: SpringerWein Verlag, 1998)

Chuen, Lam Kam. *Feng Shui Handbook* (New York: Henry Holt and Co., 1996)

Curl, James Stevens. *Oxford Dictionary of Architecture* (Oxford: Oxford University Press, 1999)

Greeves, Lydia and Michael Trinick. *The National Trust Guide* (New York: Weidenfeld & Nicolson, 1989)

Hale, Gill. *The Feng Shui Garden* (Pownal, Vt.: Storey Books, 1998)

Hopkins, E. Washburn. *Epic Mythology* (Delhi: Motilal Banarsidass, 1974)

Meena, V. *Madurai* (Cape Comorin: Harikumari Arts, n.d.)

Mercatante, Anthony S. *The Magic Garden* (New York: Harper & Row, 1976)

Michell, John. *The Traveler's Key to Sacred England* (New York: Alfred A. Knopf, 1988)

Mitchell, George, ed., *Architecture in the Islamic World* (New York: Thames and Hudson, 1995)

Moore, Charles W. *Water and Architecture*, op. cit. (See Ch 2. Bibliography)

New Catholic Encyclopedia, Vols. 3, 5 (Washington, D.C.: Catholic University of America, 1980)

New Werner Twentieth Century Edition of the Encyclopaedia Britannica, Vol. 9 (Akron, Ohio: The Werner Company, 1906)

Paccard, André. *Traditional Islamic Craft in Moroccan Architecture*, Vol. 2 (St. Jorioz: Editions Atelier 74, 1980)

Plumptre, George. *The Water Garden* (London: Thames and Hudson, 1993)

Post, Steven. *The Modern Book of Feng Shui* (New York: Dell Publishing, 1998)

Robinson, Peter. *The Water Garden* (New York: Sterling Publishing Co., 1995)

Slocum, Perry D. and Peter Robinson. *Water Gardening* (Portland, Ore.: Timber Press, Inc., 1996)

Sturgis, Russell. *A Dictionary of Architecture and Building* (New York: The Macmillan Co., 1902)

Swan, James A., ed., *The Power of Place* (Wheaton, Ill.: Quest Books, 1991)

Toy, Maggie, ed., *Architecture & Water* (London: Academy Editions, 1995)

Tricker, William. *The Water Garden* (New York: A. T. De La Mare Printing and Publishing Company, 1897)

Walters, Derek. *The Feng Shui Handbook* (London: Aquarian Press, 1991)

Waring, Philippa. *The Feng Shui of Gardening* (London: Souvenir Press, 1998)

Yang, Martin C. *A Chinese Village* (New York: Columbia University Press, 1965)

5. CLEANSING

Aaland, Mikkel. *Sweat* (Santa Barbara, Calif.: Capra Press, 1978)

Bakhtiar, Laleh. *Encyclopedia of Islamic Law* (Chicago: ABC International Group, 1996)

Bensen, Matthew. *A Dictionary of the Roman Empire* (New York: Oxford University Press, 1991)

Birnbaum, Philip. *Encyclopedia of Jewish Concepts* (Rockaway Beach, N.Y.: Hebrew Publishing Co., 1995)

Boyle, Robert H. *The Hudson River* (New York: W. W. Norton & Co., 1979)

Chapko, Chetty, ed., *About the Sweat Lodge and Its Use* (Discussion Committee of Pine Arbor Tribal Town, 1997)

Croutier, Alev Lytle. *Taking the Waters* (New York: Abbeville Press, 1992)

Elaide, Mircea, ed., *The Encyclopedia of Religion*, Vols. 5, 12 (New York: Macmillan Publishing Company, 1987)

Encyclopedia Judaica, Vols. 2, 11 (Jerusalem: Encyclopedia Judaica, 1972)

Foy, F. A. and Rose Avato. *Our Sunday Visitor's Catholic Almanac* (Huntington, Ind.: Our Sunday Visitor, 1998)

Hastings, James, ed., *Encyclopedia of Religion and Ethics*, op. cit., Vol. 6 (New York: Charles Scribner's Sons, 1951)

Johnson, Kevin Orlin. *Expressions of Catholic Faith* (New York: Ballantine Books, 1994)

Lame Dear, Archie Fire, and Richard Erdoes. *Gift of Power* (Santa Fe, N.M.: Bear & Company, 1992)

New Catholic Encyclopedia, Vol. 12 (Washington, D.C.: Catholic University of America, 1980)

6. HEALING

Altman, Nathaniel. *Healing Springs* (Rochester, Vt.: Healing Arts Press, 2000)

Brockman, Norbert C. *Encyclopedia of Sacred Sites* (Santa Barbara, Calif.: ABC-CLIO, 1997)

Buchman, Dian Dincin. *The Complete Book of Water Therapy* (New Canaan, Conn.: Keats Publishing, Inc., 1994)

Canfield, William. *The Legends of the Iroquois* (Port Washington, N.Y.: Ira J. Friedman, Inc., 1971)

Chapelle, Francis H. *The Hidden Sea* (Tucson, Ariz.: Geoscience Press, 1997)

Duckett, Eleanor Shipley. *The Gateway to the Middle Ages: Monasticism* (Ann Arbor: The University of Michigan Press, 1988)

Epstein, Donald M., et. al., *The 12 Stages of Healing* (San Rafael, Calif.: Amber-Allen Publishing/New World Library, 1994)

Fujinami, Goichi. *Hot Springs in Japan* (Tokyo: Japanese Government Railways, 1936)

Green, Miranda. *Celtic Goddesses* (New York: George Braziller, 1996)

Green, Miranda. *Dictionary of Celtic Myth and Legend* (London: Thames and Hudson, 1992)

Grimal, Pierre. *The Dictionary of Classical Mythology* (Oxford: Blackwell Publishers, 1996)

Kersley, George. "The History of Spas," *Journal of the Royal Society of Health,* 109, No. 1 (February 1989)

Klages, Ellen. *Harbin Hot Springs: Healing Waters Sacred Land* (Middletown, Calif.: Harbin Springs Publishing, 1993)

Kunz, Dora, ed., *Spiritual Aspects of the Healing Arts* (Wheaton, Ill.: Quest Books, 1985)

Lund, John W. "Hot Springs, Arkansas," *Geo-Heat Center Quarterly Bulletin* 14, No. 4 (March 1993)

Matthews, John, ed., *The Druid Source Book* (London: Blandford, 1996)

Michell, John. *The Traveler's Key to Sacred England* (New York: Alfred A. Knopf, 1988)

Oshima, Yoshio. *Thermalism in Japan* (Tokyo: The Forum on Thermalism in Japan, 1988)

Palmer, Martin and Nigel Palmer. *The Spiritual Traveler: England, Scotland, Wales* (Mahwah, N.J.: HiddenSpring, 2000)

Porter, Roy, ed., *The Medical History of Waters and Spas* (London: Wellcome Institute for the History of Medicine, 1990)

Spence, Lewis. *Myths and Legends: North American Indians* (New York: Avenel Books, 1986)

Stewart, R. J. *Celtic Goddesses* (London: Blandford, 1990)

Walsh, William S. *Curiosities of Popular Customs* (Philadelphia: J. B. Lippincott Co., 1925)

7. INITIATION

Bailey, Alice A. *Initiation, Human and Solar* (New York: Lucifer Publishing Co., 1922)

Blofeld, John. *Bodhisattva of Compassion* (Boston: Shambhala Publications, Inc., 1977)

The Catholic Encyclopedia, Vol. 7 (New York: Robert Appleton Company, 1910)

The Columbia Encyclopedia, 5th Edition (New York: Columbia University Press, 1993)

Bibliography

Evans-Wentz, W. Y. *Cuchama and Sacred Mountains* (Athens, Ohio: Swallow Press/Ohio University Press, 1981)

Getty, Alice. *The Gods of Northern Buddhism* (Rutland, Vt.: Charles E. Tuttle Co., 1962)

Govinda, Lama Anagarika. *The Way of the White Clouds* (London: Hutchinson & Co., 1966)

Hoskin, John. *The Supernatural in Thai Life* (Bangkok: The Tamarind Press, 1993)

Johnson, Kevin. *Expressions of Catholic Faith* (New York: Ballantine Books, 1994)

Lewis, Davis, trans., *The Life of St. Teresa of Jesus* (London: Thomas Baker, 1916)

Mackenzie, Donald A. *Myths of Pre-Columbian America* (Mineola, N.Y.: Dover Publications, Inc., 1996)

New Catholic Encyclopedia, Vols. 2, 5 (Washington, D.C.: Catholic University of America, 1980)

Paul, Diana Y. *Women in Buddhism* (Berkeley: Asian Humanities Press, 1979)

Powers, William K. *Oglala Religion* (Lincoln: University of Nebraska Press, 1977)

Ranger, T. O. and Isaria Kimambo. *The Historical Study of African Religion* (Berkeley: University of California Press, 1972)

Somé, Malidoma Patrice. *The Healing Wisdom of Africa* (New York: Jeremy P. Tarcher/Putnam, 1998)

Somé, Malidoma Patrice. *Of Water and the Spirit* (New York: Jeremy P. Tarcher/Putnam, 1994)

Unsworth, Tim. "Holy Waters Run Deep," *U.S. Catholic* 61 (February 1996)

8. WISDOM

Altman, Nathaniel. *The Deva Handbook: How to Work With Nature's Subtle Energies* (Rochester, Vt.: Destiny Books, 1995)

Andrews, Tamara. *Legends of the Earth, Sea and Sky* (Santa Barbara, Calif.: ABC-CLIO, 1998)

Arroyo, Stephen. *Astrology, Psychology and the Four Elements* (Davis, Calif.: CRCS Publications, 1975)

Bangs, Richard. *Islandgods* (Dallas: Taylor Publishing Co., 1991)

Bearak, Barry. "When Hindus Brave a Big Crush for a Little Dip," *New York Times,* January 25, 2001

Blofeld, John. *The Wheel of Life* (Berkeley: Shambhala, 1972)

Briggs, Katherine M. *A Dictionary of British Folk-Tales in the British Language,* Vol. 2 (London: Routledge & Kegan Paul, 1971)

Davis, William Stearns. *A Day in Old Athens* (New York: Biblo and Tannen, 1960)

Donin, Hayim Halevy. *To Be a Jew* (New York: Basic Books, 1972)

Duckett, Eleanor Shipley. *The Gateway to the Middle Ages: Monasticism* (Ann Arbor: The University of Michigan Press, 1988)

Eliade, Mircea. *The Encyclopedia of Religion,* Vol. 11 (New York: Macmillan Publishing Company, 1987)

Freeman, Mara. "Sacred Waters, Holy Wells," *Parabola,* Spring 1995

Gray, Louis Herbert, ed., *The Mythology of All Races,* Vols. 1, 2, 3 (New York: Cooper Square Publishers, Inc., 1964)

Green, Marian. *The Elements of Natural Magic* (Shaftsbury: Element Books, 1989)

Harpur, James. *The Miracles of Jesus* (Pleasantville, N.Y.: Reader's Digest Association, 1997)

Hastings, James, ed., *The Encyclopedia of Religion and Ethics,* Vol. 4 (New York: Charles Scribner's Sons, 1951)

Hodson, Geoffrey. *Hidden Wisdom in the Holy Bible,* Vol. 2 (Wheaton, Ill.: Quest Books, 1994)

Jones, Francis. *The Holy Wells of Wales* (Cardiff: University of Wales Press, 1954)

Kennedy, Patrick. *The Legendary Fictions of the Irish Celts* (New York: Benjamin Blom, 1866)

Landman, Isaac, ed., *The Universal Jewish Encyclopedia,* Vol. 10 (New York: Ktav Publishing House, 1969)

Matthews, John. *The Celtic Shaman's Pack* (Shaftsbury: Element Books, 1995)

Michell, John. *The Traveler's Key to Sacred England* (New York: Alfred A. Knopf, 1988)

New Catholic Encyclopedia, Vols. 11, 12 (Washington, D.C.: Catholic University of America, 1980)

Palmer, Martin and Nigel Palmer. *The Spiritual Traveler: England, Scotland, Wales* (Mahwah, N.J.: HiddenSpring, 2000)

Roget, Eugene. *Fontaines sacrées et saintes guérisseurs [Sacred Wells and Healing Saints]* (Lucon: Jean Paul Gisserot, 1994)

Rolleston, T. W. *Celtic Myths and Legends* (New York: Dover Publications, 1990)

Rosa, José Alberto and Nathaniel Altman. *Power Spots* (Wellingborough: The Aquarian Press, 1986)

Spence, Lewis. *The Fairy Tradition in Britain* (London: Rider and Company, 1948)

Waite, Arthur Edward. *The Pictorial Key to the Tarot* (Stamford, Conn.: U.S. Games Systems, Inc., 1995)

Westwood, Jennifer. *Sacred Journeys* (London: Gaia Books, 1997)

Wilson, A. N. *Jesus* (New York: W. W. Norton &. Co., 1992)

9. ENCHANTMENT

Altman, Nathaniel. *The Deva Handbook: How to Work with Nature's Subtle Energies* (Rochester, Vt.: Destiny Books, 1995)

Boyer, Carl B. *The Rainbow* (Princeton: Princeton University Press, 1987)

Dolfyn. *Shamanism and Sacred Ecology: Healing the Earth as We Heal Ourselves* (Oakland. Calif.: Earthspirit Inc., 1991)

Graetz, Heinrich. *History of the Jews,* Vol. 2 (Philadelphia: The Jewish Publication Society of America, 1946)

Jones, Francis. *The Holy Wells of Wales* (Cardiff: University of Wales Press, 1954)

May, Herbert and Bruce Metzger, eds., *The New Oxford Annotated Bible* (New York: Oxford University Press 1973)

Perkins, John. *The World Is as You Dream It* (Rochester, Vt.: Destiny Books, 1994)

Rappoport, Angelo S. *The Folklore of the Jews* (London: The Soncino Press, 1937)

Rosa, José Alberto and Nathaniel Altman. *Power Spots* (Wellingborough: The Aquarian Press, 1986)

Singer, Isadore, ed., *The Jewish Encyclopedia*, Vol. 12 (New York: Ktav Publishing House, 1905)

Wydra, Nancilee. *Designing Your Happiness* (Torrance, Calif.: Heian International, Inc., 1995)

Zvi Werblowsky, R. J. and G. Wigoder, eds., *The Oxford Dictionary of the Jewish Religion* (New York: Oxford University Press, 1997)

10. PROTECTING THE WATERS

de Villiers, Marq. *Water* (Boston: Houghton Mifflin Company, 2000)

"John Paul's Lenten message: 'Water's sacred; protect it.'" *National Catholic Reporter* 29, No. 16 (19 February 1993)

Rockefeller, Steven and John C. Elder, eds., *Spirit and Nature: Why the Environment Is a Religious Issue* (Boston: Beacon Press, 1992)

Sullivan, Robert. "River, Interrupted," *Conde Nast Traveler*, January 2001

INDEX

ACKNOWLEDGMENTS

The author wishes to thank Daniel Entin, Director of the Nicholas Roerich Museum in New York City for kind permission to reproduce two of Nicholas Roerich's paintings, and the Bibliothèque Nationale du Québec in Montréal for permission to reproduce graphics from its extensive print and post card collection. An extensive effort has been made to verify the rights of other graphics used in this book. If any required acknowledgments have been omitted, or any rights overlooked, it is unintentional and forgiveness is requested. If notified, the author will be happy to rectify any omissions in future editions. Finally, he wishes to thank Jan-Erik Guerth, Editorial Director at HiddenSpring, for his tireless enthusiasm, wise counsel, and editorial expertise.

PICTURE CREDITS

Page 14: The Nile at Aswan
From Robichon and Varille, *En Egypte*, 1937. Photo by Roger Viollet.

Page 19: Lenape creation myth
After Kraft and Kraft, *The Indians of Lenapehoking*. Drawing by Igor Zevin.

Page 23: Bionnassay Glacier, France
Unknown origin

Page 25: Sea serpent
Unknown origin

Page 27: The World according to Homer
From Gayley, *Classic Myths in English Literature*, 1893.

Page 32: Inuit igloo
Unknown origin

Page 36: Chalchiuhtlicue as fish goddess in water descending to first man and woman, survivors of a deluge *(Codex Vaticanus A)*
From Mackenzie, *Myths of Pre-Columbian America*.

Page 43: Doing laundry, Taxco, Mexico
Unknown origin

Page 45: Tree in autumn, China
From *A Journey Through China*.

Page 53: Falls at the Paper Mill Dam, Saguenay River, Québec
Reprinted courtesy of the Bibliothèque nationale du Québec.

Page 55: Rice paddy, Fengyuen, Taiwan
Photo by Nathaniel Altman.

Page 59: Returning from sea-fishing, Japan, 1863
From Alcock, *The Capital of the Tycoon: A Narrative of Three Years' Residence in Japan*, 1863.

Page 62: Flood time on the Nile
Unknown origin

Page 66: Sacred Lake at Temple of Amon-Re, Karnak
From Baldwin, *Egyptian Architecture as Cultural Expression.*

Page 68: Boats made of papyrus reeds
From Peake and Fleur, *Peasants & Potters.*

Page 69: Village of Fayoum
From Robichon and Varille, *En Egypte,* 1937.

Page 70: Building the old Aswan Dam, 1936
From *L'Illustration,* July 9, 1932.

Page 73: Aqueduct near Querétaro, Mexico
From Stoddard, *Glimpses of the World.*

Page 79: *Thursday* by W. Dendy Sadler
Unknown origin

Page 80: Fishing in Lake Patzcuaro, Mexico
Unknown origin

Page 82: Saint Christopher carrying the child Jesus
From Jameson, *Sacred and Legendary Art,* vol. 2.

Page 83: Crossing the river to Odawara
From Alcock, *The Capital of the Tycoon: A Narrative of Three Years' Residence in Japan,* 1863.

Page 86: Ponte S. Trinita and Ponte Vecchio, Florence
From Brangwyn and Barman, *The Bridge.* Drawing by Frank Brangwyn.

Page 94: Taj Mahal, Agra
Unknown origin

Page 97: Sizilin Garden, Suzhou, China
From *A Journey Through China.*

Page 98: Bridge in the Japanese Garden, Huntington Library, California
Unknown origin

Page 101: Sacred Bridge (Shinkyo), Nikko, Japan
Unknown origin

Page 108: Sacred well, Arima Onsen, Japan
Photograph by Nathaniel Altman.

Page 111: The Golden Lotus Tank, Madurai
Unknown origin

Page 112: The Golden Temple, Amritsar
From Caine, *Picturesque India*. Drawing by John Pedder.

Page 123: Aquae Sulis (today's Bath) in England, 43 C.E.
Reprinted courtesy of Bath Archeological Trust.

Page 125: Monks bathing (during the Middle Ages)
Reprinted courtest of the Bibliothéque nationale du Québec.

Page 131: The Jordan River at the site where Jesus is said to have been baptized
From Grober, *Palestine and Syria*, 1926.

Page 137: The Burning Ghats, Benares, 1892
From Stoddard, *Glimpses of the World*.

Page 141: Native American sweat lodge
Unknown origin

Page 146: The spa in Wiesbaden, Germany
Unknown origin

Page 155: Small shrine near Umijigoku Springs, Beppu, Japan
Unknown origin

Page 159: Bathing at Hot Springs, Florida, 1968
Unknown origin

Page 162: Taking water from the grotto at Lourdes
Unknown origin

Page 163: Carrying water from Mary's Well, Nazareth
From Grober, *Palestine and Syria*, 1926.

Page 171: The baptism of Jesus
Reprinted courtesy of the Bibliothèque nationale du Québec.

Page 173: Baptismal font, Aquileia, Italy
Reprinted courtesy of the Bibliothèque nationale du Québec.

Page 179: Kalachakra mandala
Unknown origin

Page 187: Jacob's Well, Sychar
From Grober, *Palestine and Syria*, 1926.

Page 190: The Spring of Moses in the Sinai

From Robichon and Varille, *En Egypte,* 1937. Photo by
Andre Vigneau.

Page 195: The Star

From Waite, *The Pictorial Key to the Tarot,* 1910.

Page 196: The Ace of Cups

From Waite, *The Pictorial Key to the Tarot,* 1910.

Page 199: *Brahmaputra* by Nicholas Roerich (1945)

Reprinted courtesy of the Nicholas Roerich Museum, New York.
All rights reserved.

Page 206: *Beneath the Wave off Kanagawa* by Katsushika Hokusai (1827)

Unknown origin

Page 208: Montmorency Falls, near Québec City

From Heriot, *Travels Through the Canadas,* 1807. Reprinted courtesy
of the Bibliothèque nationale du Québec.

Page 209: Niagara Falls

From Weld, *Voyage au Canada,* 1802. Reprinted courtesy of the
Bibliothèque nationale du Québec.

Page 210: Beaver Meadow Falls, Lake Placid, New York

Unknown origin

Page 211: Big waves at Santa Barbara, California

Unknown origin

Page 217: Dragon boat race, Singapore

Unknown origin

Page 219: Dai Water Festival

From *A Journey Through China.*

Page 223: At the head of the slide, Dufferin Terrace, Québec City

Reprinted courtesy of the Bibliothèque nationale du Québec.

Page 226: *Lotus* by Nicholas Roerich (1933)

Reprinted courtesy of the Nicholas Roerich Museum, New York.
All rights reserved.

Page 229: Kuan Yin

Unknown origin

Sacred Water

Page 234: Wuxia Gorge of the Three Gorges of the Yangtze River
From *A Journey Through China.*

Page 237: Latone Basin and Fountain, Park of Versailles, France
Unknown origin

Page 241: The water carriers, San Pedro Atitlán, Guatemala
Unknown origin